Utah National Parks

Arches & Canyonlands Day Hikes

by Anne and Mike Poe

Cover photo by Anne Poe
Shafer Viewpoint at Island in the Sky, Canyonlands National Park

Utah National Parks
Arches & Canyonlands Day Hikes

by Anne and Mike Poe

Published by Take A Hike Guidebooks
848 N Rainbow Blvd. #1804
Las Vegas, NV 89107

To order books, email: takeahikeguidebooks@gmail.com

Trail conditions change frequently in the backcountry due to many factors. We appreciate hiker's comments and feedback. For trail updates, corrections, feedback or comments, go to:
facebook.com/takeahikeguidebooks

If you are unhappy in any way with this book, please contact us at takeahikeguidebooks@gmail.com and we will do our best to meet your needs.

Copyright © 2013 by Take A Hike Guidebooks
ISBN 978-0-9829766-3-0

Book Layout & Cover Design   Kelly Jo Tullberg, KJ Graphic Design

Base Maps Created with Garmin Basecamp
Back Cover Map Courtesy of fiveutahparks.com

Map Design	Anne Poe
Photography	Anne and Mike Poe
Assistant Researchers	Rozanne Evans and Al Lowande
	Ridgway, Colorado

Other books by Anne and Mike Poe
    Crested Butte Colorado 65 Scenic Day Hikes 2012
    Southwest Colorado High Country Day Hikes 2012
    On Our Own: A Bicycling Adventure in Southeast Asia 2011

Printed in China by Everbest Printing Co. through Four Colour Print Group

All rights reserved. No part of this book may be reproduced or utilized in any form by any means, electronic or mechanical, including photocopying and recording, or by any information storage and retrieval system, without the prior written permission by the copyright owner unless such copying is expressly permitted by federal copyright law.

Dedication

To Shirley
& In Memory of Larry
Friends Forever

All Hikes Chart

Utah National Parks: Arches & Canyonlands Day Hikes

Hike	Name	Circuit	Difficulty	Hiking Miles	Elevation Gain (ft)	Driving Miles	Page
Arches National Park						**TH Map pg. 22**	
1	Park Avenue	Shuttle		1.00	+62	2.30	24
	La Sal Mountains Viewpoint					2.60	28
	Courthouse Towers Viewpoint					3.60	30
	Petrified Dunes Viewpoint					5.90	32
2	Balanced Rock	Loop		0.30	+55	8.80	34
	Garden of the Eden Viewpoint					10.00	36
3a	The Windows Arches Loop	Loop		0.70	+222	11.50	38
3b	The Windows Primitive Loop	Loop		1.10	+294	11.50	
4	Double Arch	RT		1.00	+41	11.50	42
	Panorama Point					10.10	44
5	Delicate Arch	RT		3.00	+690	13.20	46
6a	Delicate Arch Lower Viewpoint	RT		200 yds	+10	14.20	50
6b	Delicate Arch Upper Viewpoint	RT		1.00	+325	14.20	
	Salt Valley Overlook					13.60	52
	Fiery Furnace Overlook					13.80	54
7	Fiery Furnace	RT		2.00	Varies	13.80	56
8a	Sand Dune Arch	RT		0.36	+124	15.70	58
8b	Sand Dune Arch Loop	Loop		2.80	+333	15.70	
9	Skyline Arch	RT		0.50	+52	16.40	64
10a	Devil's Garden: Landscape Arch	RT		3.02	+260	17.40	66
10b	Devil's Garden: Double O Arch	RT		5.90	+1552	17.40	
10c	Devil's Garden: Primitive Loop	Loop		6.69	+1507	17.40	
11	Tower Arch	RT		2.66	+723	24.40	72
Island in the Sky Canyonlands National Park						**TH Map pg. 80**	
12a	The Neck to Taylor Canyon Viewpoint	RT		4.50	+1308	0.40	82
12b	The Neck Loop	Loop		5.80	+1547	0.40	
13	Schafer Viewpoint Trail	RT		0.20	+22	0.40	88
	Schafer Trail Overlook					0.80	90
14a	Lathrop to Overlook	RT		4.30	+359	1.90	92
14b	Lathrop to Top of Big Descent	RT		6.00	+1644	1.90	
14c	Lathrop to White Rim Road	RT		10.50	+2849	1.90	
15	Mesa Arch	Loop		0.65	+115	5.90	96
	Green River Overlook					7.50	98
16a	Aztec Butte 1st Butte	RT		0.95	+134	6.70	100

Devil's Garden Primitive Trail Loop, Hike 10C

All Hikes Chart

Hike	Name	Circuit	Difficulty	Hiking Miles	Elevation Gain (ft)	Driving Miles	Page
Island in the Sky Canyonlands National Park, cont.							
16b	Aztec Butte Both Buttes	RT		1.61	+348	6.70	100
17a	Wilhite to Edge of Cliffs	RT		2.56	+408	8.00	106
17b	Wilhite to Lunch Spot	RT		4.98	+1621	8.00	
17c	Wilhite to White Rim Road	RT		11.64	+2775	8.00	
18a	Alcove Springs to Alcove Amphitheater	RT		2.00	+875	9.50	112
18b	Alcove Springs to Taylor Canyon Road	RT		11.00	+2104	9.50	
19	Whale Rock	RT		1.00	+223	9.90	116
20	Syncline Loop	Loop		8.50	+2949	10.70	118
21a	Upheaval Dome 1st Overlook	RT		0.60	+158	10.70	124
21b	Upheaval Dome 2nd Overlook	RT		1.60	+496	10.70	
22a	Murphy Hogback to Cliffs	RT		2.00	+228	8.20	128
22b	Murphy Hogback to Murphy Camp	RT		9.54	+2104	8.20	
22c	Murphy Hogback Loop	Loop		10.00	+2258	8.20	
23	Murphy Viewpoint Trail	RT		3.40	+292	8.20	132
Buck Canyon Overlook						9.00	134
24	Gooseberry	RT		5.40	+1457	10.80	136
25	White Rim Overlook Trail	RT		1.50	+135	10.80	140
26	Grandview Trail	RT		2.00	+498	12.00	142
Grandview Point Overlook						12.00	144
Needles Canyonlands National Park						**TH Map pg. 148**	
27	Roadside Ruin	Loop		0.30	+10	0.60	150
28	Cave Spring	Loop		0.70	+72	3.10	152
29a	Paul Bunyan's Potty	RT		6.60	+121	3.00	154
29b	Tower Ruin	RT		9.20	+183	3.00	
30a	Castle Arch	RT		16.80	+450	3.00	158
30b	Fortress Arch	RT		18.00	+507	3.00	
Wooden Shoe Overlook						2.30	162
31	Pot Hole Point	Loop		0.60	+45	5.00	164
32	Slickrock Foot Trail	Loop		2.50	+304	6.30	166
Big Spring Canyon Overlook						6.40	170
33	Confluence Overlook Trail (Any Distance)	RT		10.00	+784	6.40	172
34a	Peekaboo Trail to Saddle	RT		3.50	+378	4.00	178
34b	Peekaboo Trail to 1st Peekaboo	RT		7.70	+1467	4.00	
34c	Peekaboo Trail to Peekaboo Camp	RT		10.00	+2066	4.00	

All Hikes Chart

Needles Canyonlands National Park, cont.

Hike	Name	Circuit	Difficulty	Hiking Miles	Elevation Gain (ft)	Driving Miles	Page
35	Squaw Canyon / Big Springs Canyon Loop	Loop		7.10	+1181	4.00	184
36	Big Spring / Elephant Canyon Loop	Loop		10.30	+2259	4.00	188
37	Squaw Canyon / Lost Canyon Loop	Loop		8.60	+1352	4.00	194
38	Elephant Hill / Squaw Flat CG	Shuttle		4.70	+960	6.00	202
39	Druid Arch	RT		9.60	+1775	6.00	206
40a	Chesler Overlook	RT		5.40	+1700	6.00	212
40b	Chesler Loop	Loop		10.30	+2548	6.00	
41	Devil's Kitchen Loop	Loop		10.90	+2614	6.00	220
42a	Squaw Flats Campground Loop A	Loop		1.20	+253	6.00	230
42b	Squaw Flats Campground Loop B	Loop		1.55	+250	6.00	
42c	Squaw Flats Campground Loop A to B	Loop		1.15	+206	6.00	

Mesa Arch, Hike 15

Numerous park trails have ladders.

Table of Contents

Dedication	3
All Hikes Chart	4-7
Introduction	**10-12**
Why Hike Arches & Canyonlands	10
Where are Arches & Canyonlands	11
Why This Guidebook is Different	12
How to Use this Guide	**13-15**
Find the Hikes You Want	13
Hike Options	13
Difficulty Ratings	13
Hiking Times	14
Summary Charts	14
How We Obtain Trail Data	14
Symbols	14
Carry This Guide	15
Other Considerations	**16-17**
Temperatures	16
Water	16
Don't Bust the Crust!	17
Archeological Sites	17
Arches National Park	**18-75**
Introduction	18
Map of All Trailheads	22
Hikes 1-11	24
Island in the Sky District, Canyonlands National Park	**76-145**
Introduction	76
Map of All Trailheads	80
Hikes 12-26	82
Needles District, Canyonlands National Park	**146-235**
Introduction	146
Map of All Trailheads	148
Hikes 27-42	150
Appendix A: Entrance Fees, Addresses and Park Regulations	236
Appendix B: Camping	237
Appendix C: Backcountry Regulations, Permits and Camping	241
Meet the Authors	243

Introduction

Why Hike Arches & Canyonlands

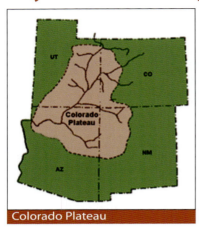
Colorado Plateau

The Colorado Plateau is a physical geological region that spreads across western Colorado, southern and eastern Utah, northern Arizona, and northwestern New Mexico. It has been home to the ancient and mysterious Anasazi, and to modern day cowboy and Indian cultures. It is presently home to the greatest concentration of National Parks in the United States. Centered primarily on the Four Corners region, it covers about 130,000 square miles. The average elevation of the plateau is 5000 feet; it is described as high desert. Most of the area is drained by the Colorado and Green Rivers.

Wind and water have played a major role in the formation of both Arches and Canyonlands. Wind, like sandpaper, scrapes away at the softer rock formations, sculpting like an artist; water penetrates porous rock, freezes and breaks it apart. The result is massive buttes, delicate spires, amazing arches, narrow slot canyons, and whale fins decorating a desert landscape of sand, slickrock and biological crust. Desert flowers bloom in spring; junipers dominate the tree world; small lizards and rabbits the animal world.

This is a landscape begging to be explored. Traveling by foot through it, in it and across it has ancient roots indeed. Now, there is a marvelous network of trails for the modern explorer. That's you!

A local resident

Pear Cactus Flowers show off in the spring

The hiking trails in Arches and Canyonlands overlook, descend, ascend, and wind in and around this stunning landscape providing an album of photographs waiting to be shot. Some trails are spacious, wide paths of man-made packed gravel. Some cross slickrock with rock cairns for guidance; some require negotiating over, around, down and up boulders and rock ledges, cliffs, and even ladders. Some feel intimate; others feel overwhelmingly vast. There are very easy and very challenging trails; there is something to inspire every type of hiker. Come and see for yourself.

Where are Arches & Canyonlands

Moab, Utah, a vibrant, adventure and service oriented town in southeastern Utah is a great place to start and plan your time in Arches and Canyonlands. It is close to the areas detailed in this book. The Visitor Center on Center Street is a gold mine of helpful information and offers a grand selection of maps, guides, historical and photo books, postcards…the list goes on. Motels, restaurants, campsites abound. Guided river, bicycle, and jeep tours and rentals make Moab a leader in adventure activities. Camping in the area is abundant, from full amenity RV parks, to primitive camping on BLM land. See appendix B for more information.

Map Courtesy of fiveutahparks.com

Moab, however, is itself remote as travel distances and time are measured. Green River, Utah (50 miles) and Grand Junction, Colorado (110 miles) both have Amtrak train service and nationwide bus service. Moab, Grand Junction and Salt Lake City (236 miles) have commercial air service. Still, most visitors come in their own vehicle or motor home. Many out of country visitors rent a camper unit.

- Arches Park is just 4.4 miles north of Center Street Visitor Center in Moab via Hwy 191.
- Island in the Sky District of Canyonlands National Park is 10.7 miles north of Center Street Visitor Center in Moab via Hwy 191 and west 25 miles via SR313.
- The Needles District of Canyonlands National Park is 40 miles south of Moab on Hwy 191 and west 35 miles on SR211. Watch for the National Park sign opposite Church Rock on Hwy 191. Do not turn off by mistake on Needles Overlook Road which is just a few miles north of the correct junction.

Why This Guidebook is Different

- Guidebooks should stimulate. Pictures are worth more than a thousand words. Color pictures equal a million. You see color when you hike. The colors in Arches and Canyonlands are sublime and thrilling. Massive rock walls, spires, and buttes in shades of red, purple, beige and white stand firmly outlined by the blue sky. The vast open space melts into the haze of extreme distance. In our opinion, such magic cannot be adequately

La Sal Mountains from Big Spring Trail, Hike 35

portrayed through black and white photography. Our gallery of photos shows you, in color, what you can expect to see on the trail and why you might like to go and enjoy it in person
- Guidebooks should guide. They should provide a variety of information for all levels of hikers so they can choose the hikes best suited and most rewarding for them
- Guidebooks should be accurate: The writers need to have hiked the trails themselves
- Guidebooks should be user friendly. Specific, important information is framed by colored boxes. It is quick and easy to find
- Guidebooks should have maps! Good maps are the essence of a good guidebook. For each area, Arches, Island in the Sky and Needles, there is an overview map with all the trailheads and scenic overlooks plotted. The trailheads are numbered, named, and colored for difficulty level for quick and easy reference. Trail mileages as well as road mileage between all points of interest are in red and black italics between arrows. Roads are designated as paved, gravel or 4WD. In addition, there is a detailed map for each hike and elevation profiles for all but the very flat hikes. The numbered colored circles on the maps correspond to circles in the text and in the Summary Chart. Good maps bring the trail to life.

How To Use This Guide

Find the Hikes You Want

The Hikes Chart is innovative. It is a complete chart that, at a glance, provides you with information to help you search for a hike that is right for you: difficulty level (shown as a particular color), total distance, shuttle, loop, or round trip hike, and elevation change are listed for every hike and option.

Hike Options

Perhaps a hike is longer than you wish to do; we suggest shorter options and recommend different, sensible return points. We explain the difficulty level and distance for such options in the Hikes Chart as well as in the general information box at the beginning of each hike. For example, hike 10, Devil's Garden, has three options listed as 10a, 10b, and 10c. You don't have to dismiss a long hike because it appears to be too far or too difficult.

Difficulty

The level of difficulty for a hike is very subjective. We use six categories to help you define for yourself how difficult the hike would be for you: total distance, difficulty rating, surface, gradient, elevation at the trailhead, and total elevation gain.

- **TOTAL DISTANCE** is expressed as the total mileage it takes to complete the round trip, the loop, or to arrive at the shuttle point.

- **DIFFICULTY RATING** is a summary assessment of the total hike that takes into consideration distance, surface conditions, gradient, and elevation gain. The categories are represented by colors and words as follows: Easy (green), Moderate (cyan), Moderately Strenuous (blue), Strenuous (orange), Very Strenuous (red).

- **SURFACE:** Are you walking on packed gravel, through deep soft sand or across slickrock. Are there high steps to negotiate, narrow ledges, use of hands to get up or down a particular place. Since no trail has the same surface conditions from start to finish, we have written a brief description of the various conditions encountered.

- **GRADIENT** affects many hikers more than distance. We divide gradient into the following categories: Easy, Moderate, Moderately Steep, Steep, and Very Steep. The various trail colors on the map represent these gradient changes as you progress on the trail.
    - **Green:** Easy Gradient. Trail climbs between 0 to 400 feet per mile.
    - **Cyan:** Moderate gradient. Trail climbs between 400 to 600feet per mile.
    - **Blue:** Moderately Steep. Trail climbs between 600 to 800 feet per mile.
    - **Orange:** Steep gradient. Trail climbs between 800 to 1,000 feet per mile.
    - **Red:** Very Steep gradient. Trail climbs over 1,000 feet per mile.

- **Yellow:** Represents connecting and other trails. It does not symbolize any gradient.

- **Trailhead Elevation:** Do you come from sea level? The average elevation of the hikes in these parks is around 5000 feet.

- **Elevation Gain:** Many hiking guides measure elevation gain by subtracting the starting elevation from the highest point. We measure total vertical gain with the use of one or two GPS devices that measure every foot of elevation gain during the entire hike. Many times this gain is greater than simple subtraction. Our figure, preceded by a plus sign, is the total amount of elevation gained from the start and back on a round trip hike, and from the start to the end on a loop or shuttle hike.

Hiking Times

Assessing hiking times is even more personal than difficulty ratings. Some folks have long strides, others like to keep a slower pace. On average, we hike 2.0 mph on easy hikes, 1.5 mph on moderate, and 1.0 on strenuous. Times stated are for the complete hike. We were in our late 60s at the time we hiked these trails.

Summary Charts

Instead of long descriptions, the Summary Chart puts all that data in one quick and easy reference.

The number in the first column in the chart, corresponds to the number in the circle on the map. The chart then lists the mileage covered to each point, elevation, and instructions on what to do when you get there.

How We Obtain Trail Data

We have hiked every trail ourselves in this book. We do not take data from pre-existing maps or other guide books as some of these sources may be outdated. Nor do we rely on the posted signs along the trails. The distance and elevation data we offer is extracted from the Garmin E-Trex Venture HC series GPS. No consumer GPS is totally accurate. In addition, no two people can hike across slickrock, or in sandy washes in the same steps. Even following cairns and other markers, our routes will be slightly different. Therefore, our mileages for a hike may disagree with pre-existing maps and books.

Symbols & Glossary

- **NPS:** National Park Service
- **BLM:** Bureau of Land Management
- **AVC:** Arches Visitor Center
- **ISVC:** Island in the Sky Visitor Center
- **NVC:** Needles Visitor Center
- **RT:** Round trip
- **TH:** Trailhead
- **CG:** Campground

- **(P)** in a yellow circle represents a place to park
- **(T)** is a pit toilet
- **(W)** is drinking water available
- **GPS Waypoints:** Numbers highlighted by a colored circle on the maps and in the text indicate points of interest, or trail junctions.
- Roads are designed as paved, gravel, or 4WD. Cars can drive the paved and gravel roads. High clearance SUVs or 4x4 vehicles are recommended on 4WD roads.

Chesler Trail in the Needles

Carry This Guide

There is a lot of information in this guidebook. It is meant to be carried with you when you hike. When you hike one trail, you may pass the routes to other hikes. We show the connecting hikes in black. This makes it easy to see how they interconnect. Your understanding and appreciation of the area will grow exponentially. It allows you to see the terrain for a future hike or change your mind and hike a different trail on the spur of the moment. You will know where that intriguing trail goes. Other hikers may inspire you to go on their favorite trail. The information you need is in your hands.

When you carry the book, you can consult the GPS Chart to know how far you have gone and how much time you may linger before turning back. You will know what to expect ahead, what is yet to see and experience.

The color coded maps give information about changing levels of gradient along the trail. Gage your fitness and assess how far you might go. Some of the long, difficult hikes have scenic beginnings that are not difficult. Consult the maps and look for green or cyan colored trails near the beginning of long hikes and go only that far.

Other Considerations

Temperatures

Summer months of June through September temperatures can average from 80 to 100 degrees Fahrenheit. July and August are the hottest. The average humidity, however, is very low. There is very little shade on many trails. A short hike through deep, soft sand can require twice the effort in this summer heat. April, May and October the temperatures range from 60 to 80 degrees Fahrenheit. This is a very busy time in the parks.

Water

Water is essential for hikers to maintain good condition. Too many day hikers convince themselves they can drink when they get back because they don't want to carry the extra weight. On a cool or cloudy day, the signs of thirst are reduced, which tempts day hikers to drink even less. Don't make these mistakes. The muscles need to flush out lactic acid while you are hiking to maintain fitness.

We recommend using a bladder system as opposed to a water bottle hidden in your pack. A bladder makes it convenient to take sips every fifteen minutes whether you feel thirsty or not. For best results, drink about 16 ounces or more for every hour of exercise. On longer hikes, we also take several small bottles of water with a sports drink mixed in. It re-hydrates, replenishes, and refuels better than water alone.

Water can be obtained at the following locations:
- Arches Visitor Center and Devil's Campground (Dispersed by spigots)
- Island in the Sky Visitor Center (Sold in bottles)
- Needles Visitor Center and Squaw Flat Campground (Dispersed by spigots)

Granary, Hike 27

Biological Soil Crusts

Don't Bust the Crust!

Biological soil crusts are present in every desert environment. They are the building blocks of life, providing nutrients for plants, holding 10 times their volume in precious water, and preventing erosion by secreting a sticky mucilage that glue soil particles together. Crusts are formed by living organisms of blue-green algae, one of the oldest known life forms. They develop exceedingly slowly. In early development, the crusts look like the surrounding soil but become darker and lumpy with maturity. One crunching step on this mature soil could take up to 250 years to repair. A single bicycle track not only kills the crust but speeds up erosion as it creates a path for water to flow.

To prevent destruction of this precious crust, stay on designated trails, hike on slickrock or in sandy washes.

Archeological Sites

There are three designations for archeological sites:
- Category 1: Sites where the public is encouraged to visit and access is well described
- Category 2: Sites that may be known by the public but are not publicized. Park Rangers do not mention these sites unless someone makes a specific inquiry to see it.
- Category 3: Sites that are not allowed in the public knowledge base

There are several category 1 sites in Arches and Canyonlands National Parks. They consist primarily of granaries and petroglyphs. Touching the artifacts aids in their destruction; oils from the human hand are corrosive. It is also against Federal law to touch rock art.

Arches National Park

Arches National Park is popular and famous all over the world for good reason. There is no other place with 2500 arches (and still counting) in one concentrated location. Arches begin their life as parts of solid and sometimes massive walls of red sandstone. Water, a most precious resource with minimum application penetrates the cracks, crevices and lesions in the rock, freezes and splits them apart. This process takes centuries. Many arches are formed by potholes on the surface where water freezes and thaws and breaks apart tiny chips of rock until a hole passes through a weak layer. That requires a lot of patience! New arches form and old arches disintegrate and fall. Famous Landscape Arch is an example of an old arch beginning its decline. Since 1991, (three pieces of rock 30, 47, and 70 feet long) have fallen from the bottom of the arch. Skyline Arch doubled in size when the bottom fell out. The huge boulders are piled high at the end of the trail. To be an official arch, the hole must be a minimum of three feet in any one direction. All over the park there is evidence of new arches about to be born. A great place to spot many of them is from the Windows Section parking lot. Just scan your eyes across the red sandstone in the area and you will see giant caves and tiny openings.

Arches Park is as much a driving park as it is a hiking one. From the entrance to the end at Devil's Garden campground is just over 17 miles. In that distance, there are 7 stunning overlooks and 6 hiking trails. Two short side roads offer another driving overlook and 4 more hikes. There is also one primitive hike in a secluded corner of the park that is little visited.

Most of Arches hikes are short and easy. Thus, they are extremely popular with folks who enjoy brief exercise in a natural environment surrounded by abundant photographic opportunities. Many a wife, husband or friend goes home with a treasured memory captured in the company of towering buttes and magnificent

Since 1991, Landscape Arch has lost big sections of rock.

arches. Spend an hour, a day or a week admiring, photographing and strolling through this amazing scenery.

- **Hike 1:** Park Avenue has wheel chair access out about 100 yards to a wonderful overlook before it descends more steeply to the bottom of a wide canyon.

- **Hike 2:** Balanced Rock is a short easy loop around a massive boulder perched on a stone pedestal.
- **Hike 3a:** Windows Arches Loop follows a wide, well constructed path up carved stone steps to three wondrous arches.
- **Hike 4:** Double Arch is very short and very easy trail to the base of two arches formed by potholes.
- **Hike 6a:** Delicate Arch Lower Viewpoint Trail offers wheelchair access to a viewing point of the beautiful Delicate Arch.
- **Hike 8a:** Sand Dune Arch is also very short and very popular with families. The arch is hidden in the narrows of a massive slot.
- **Hike 9:** Skyline Arch climbs very gently to a viewpoint at the base of a cliff. The arch is high above.
- **Hike 10a:** Devil's Garden Trail to Landscape Arch offers a wide, well groomed path to three arches in all, with a return from the famous Landscape Arch.

Because most of Arches visitors are not hard core hikers, we have tried to be careful in designating the difficulty level of trails based on the needs of the occasional

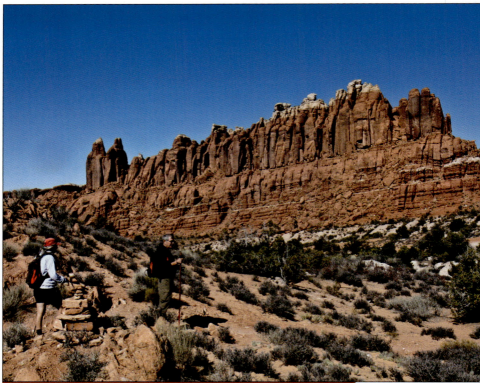

Arches National Park has more than arches to see, Hike 11.

hiker. If a hike involves a bit more steepness, or perhaps the need to negotiate over rock ledges or hike along cliff edges, we will have given the hike a Moderate or Moderately Strenuous rating. The following hikes we deemed Moderate.

- **Hike 3b:** Windows Primitive Loop has just one place where one must scramble up a ledge. In places, the trail follows rock cairns across slickrock.
- **Hike 5:** Delicate Arch requires a longer ascent up steeper slickrock. There is a wide section along the edge of a steep cliff.
- **Hike 6b:** Delicate Arch Upper Viewpoint has a steeper section with loose rock underfoot.
- **Hike 8b:** Sand Dune Arch Loop is a longer hike overall and goes through some deep sand and scrambles over bigger steps in the slickrock.
- **Hike 11:** Tower Arch is truly a primitive trail with a steep, narrow trail with big steps up at the start and sections of deep sand near the end.

There are only three hikes in all of arches we categorized as Moderately Strenuous:

- **Hike 7:** Fiery Furnace is a guided hike or requires a permit as it is a maze of dead end trails and is easy to get lost. Scrambling over boulders is most likely necessary.
- **Hike 10b:** Devil's Garden Double O Arch has many sections of steep slickrock, big steps up and down, and exposed walking along cliffs.
- **Hike 10c:** Devil's Garden Primitive Loop is long and tiring especially on a hot day. There is lots of scrambling over rock ledges, sliding down slickrock on your butt and other adventurous stuff. A fabulous hike!

Parking spaces throughout the park are limited and often are full by 10AM with enthusiastic nature lovers. A short wait, however usually finds a return hiker or photographer vacating their spot. Don't miss the overlooks; most have interpretive signs and are really fascinating. They are as much a contribution to your enjoyment as the trails.

Arches Park is about the desert and its fragile ecosystem. Water is a minimal resource and highly coveted. Visitors will find drinking water at the Arches Visitor Center and at Devil's Garden Campground. Bring your own refillable water bottles or you can buy them at the visitor center. The visitor center is also a special place to explore in itself. Maps, books photographs, postcards are well stocked items. There are displays and films on the park and its geological features. The park rangers offer friendly and knowledgeable information. Be sure to visit this marvelous resource as well. It is just .20 miles past the entrance station.

Devil's Garden Campground at the end of the Arches Road has 52 sites available on a first come, first served basis. See more details in appendix B

Arches National Park is only 4.4 miles north on Hwy 191 from the Visitor Center in Moab.

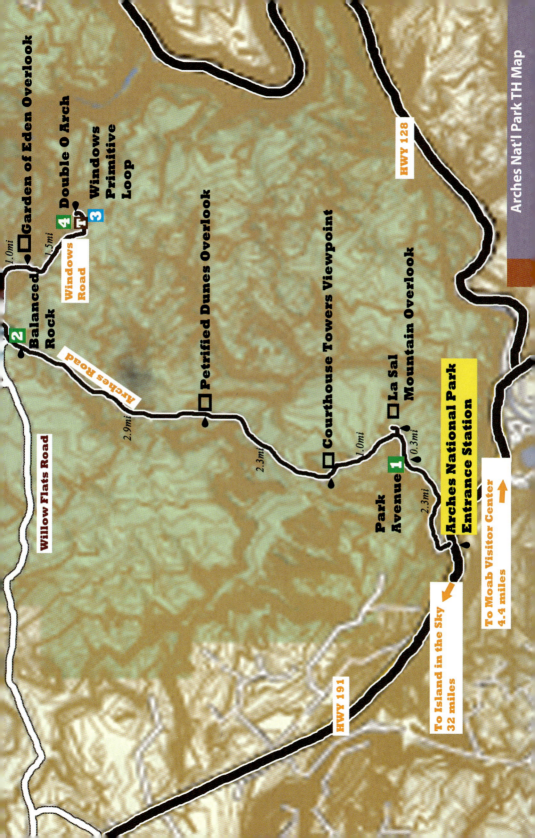

Park Avenue

Total Distance	1.0 mile to shuttle
Difficulty Rating	Easy
Surface	Short Section paved for Wheel Chair; remainder is dirt packed and slick rock
Gradient	Mostly Easy with one short Moderately Steep descent
Average Time	30 minutes
Elevations	TH: 4,512; Gain: +62 south to north; +332 north to south
Maps	Trails Illustrated #211 Arches National Park; USGS Arches National Park

View from the overlook

Summary

This is a wonderfully scenic walk through a canyon with steep, dramatic walls; nature's version of the famous New York street carved in red sandstone. There are buttes, and alcoves to explore and close up shots of the popularly photographed Three Gossips, Courthouse Towers, the Tower of Babel, Sheep Rock and The Organ. Hike from either end using a short shuttle (South to North is downhill) or hike out and back.

Directions to Trailhead

From Arches Entrance Station, drive 2.3 miles to the signed parking lot for Park Avenue. Parking spaces for small RVs. Facilities: None. For the north end shuttle,

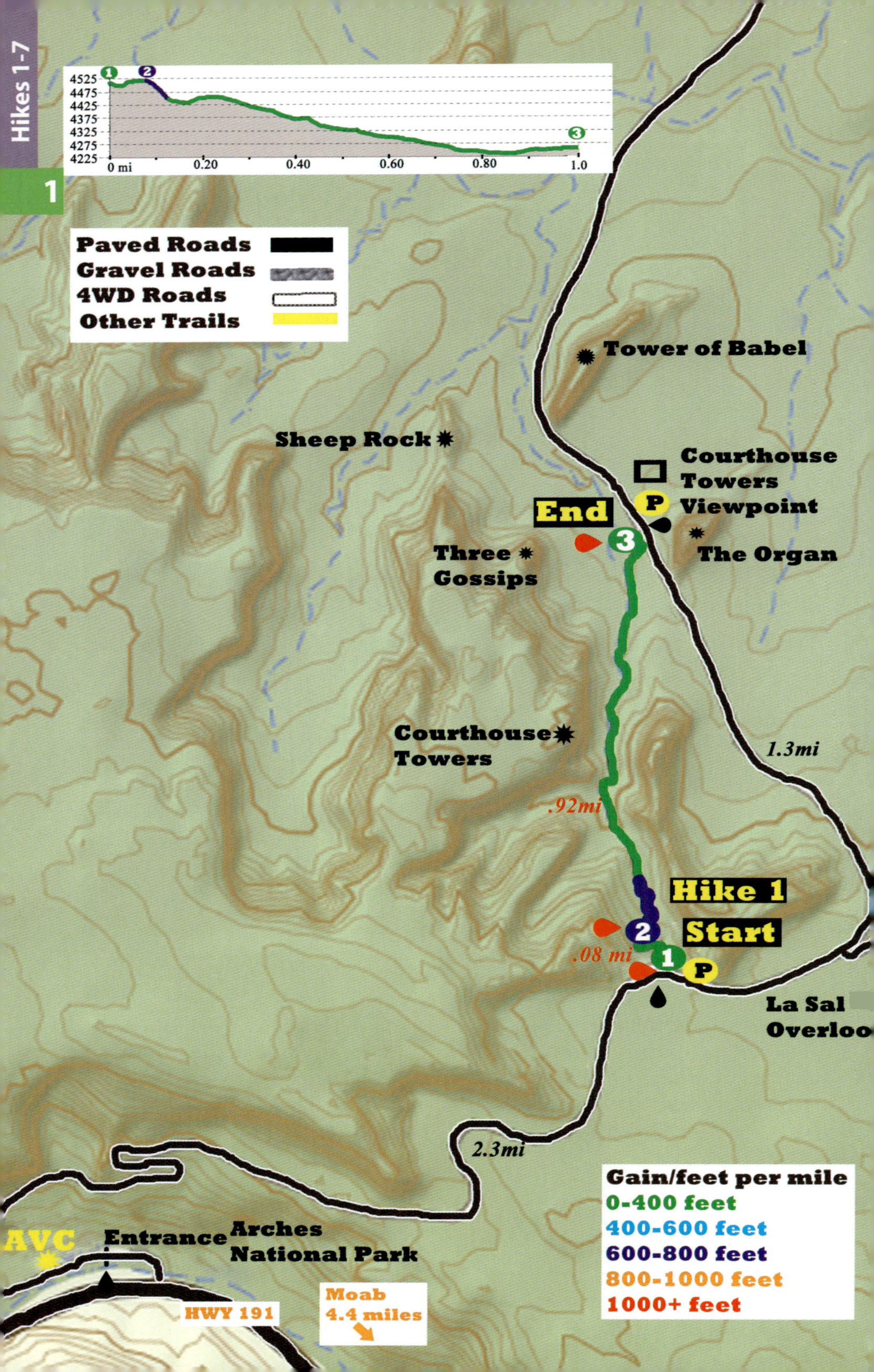

1
2
3
4525
4475
4425
4375
4325
4275
4225
0 mi
0.20
0.40
0.60
0.80
1.0
Paved Roads
Gravel Roads
4WD Roads
Other Trails
Tower of Babel
Sheep Rock
Courthouse Towers Viewpoint
P
End
3
Three Gossips
The Organ
Courthouse Towers
1.3mi
.92mi
Hike 1
Start
2
.08 mi
1
P
La Sal Overloo
2.3mi
Gain/feet per mile
0-400 feet
400-600 feet
600-800 feet
800-1000 feet
1000+ feet
AVC
Entrance
Arches National Park
HWY 191
Moab 4.4 miles

drive another 1.3 miles north on Arches Road to the Courthouse Towers Viewpoint parking lot. Trail is across the road.

Trail Description

Starting at Park Avenue parking lot, the trail is concrete for about 100 yards to a wonderful viewpoint before dropping Moderately Steeply down a narrow path to the canyon floor. The canyon is wide, the path meanders across slickrock and sand completely removed from the hustle and bustle of Arches Road.

GPS	Mile	Elevation	Comment
1	0.00	4,512'	Start Park Avenue at south end and hike downhill.
2	0.08	4,520'	End wheel chair access.
3	1.00	4,244'	End hike at Courthouse Towers Viewpoint parking lot.

Hikers on lower Park Avenue

La Sal Mountain Overlook

Stop here for wonderful views of the La Sal Mountains and of a complex of towering rocks in the Courthouse/Park Avenue area including The Three Gossips, The Organ, Courthouse Tower, Sheep Rock and the Tower of Babel. Parking lot with spaces for RVs. Interpretive signs. No facilities. Mile 2.6 from Arches Entrance Station.

La Sal Mountain Overlook

This viewpoint provides a close up of the massive towering rocks seen from the La Sal Overlook. Stand at the base of The Organ or get a close up view of the Three Gossips. This is also the shuttle pick up point for through hikers of Park Avenue. Parking lot with spaces for RV's. No facilities. Mile 3.6 from Arches Entrance Station.

Courthouse Towers Viewpoint

Petrified Dunes Overlook

Two hundred million years ago, winds from the northwest brought tons of sand into this area creating huge dunes. As other heavier soils accumulated on top, the loose sand was compressed into Navajo Sandstone rock. Eventually, water erosion took the soils away and the dunes remain. Roadside pull off with room for RV's. Interpretive signs. No facilities. Mile 5.9 from Arches Entrance Station.

Balanced Rock

Balanced Rock as seen from the road

Total Distance	0.30 mile loop
Difficulty Rating	Easy
Surface	Packed dirt & gravel wide trail
Gradient	Easy
Average Time	20 minutes
Elevations	TH: 5,038; Gain: +55 ft
Maps	Trails Illustrated #211 Arches National Park; USGS Arches National Park

Summary

Balanced Rock is an amazing natural feature: a 55 foot diameter rock is precariously balanced on a rock pedestal 128 feet high. A trail circumnavigates the rock formation allowing many surprising viewpoints. The trail is very easy and very short.

Directions to Trailhead

From Arches Entrance Gate, drive 8.8 miles to the signed parking lot for Balanced Rock. Parking spaces for small RV's. Facilities: None

Balanced Rock

Garden of Eden Viewpoint

A garden of stone flowers reaching into the sunlight. The area features many arches-to-be. Parking lot and turnaround with spaces for small RVs. No facilities. Turn right (E) on Windows Road at mile 9.0 from Arches Entrance Station and drive 1.0 more mile to signed viewpoint.

Windows Loops

3a: Windows Arches Loop

Total Distance	0.70 miles around the loop
Difficulty Rating	Easy
Surface	Packed gravel with many rock steps
Gradient	Easy to Moderate
Average Time	30 minutes
Elevations	TH: 5,146; Gain: +222
Maps	Trails Illustrated #211 Arches National Park; USGS Arches National Park

North Window

Summary
This is an extremely popular trail. The Windows Arches Trail makes a loop that visits three arches: North & South Window and Turret Arch. There are many stone steps to climb from the parking lot to visit these arches but the trail is wide and the steps are built of rock slabs and gravel. The primitive loop continues around to the back side of the Windows where you can see both of them side by side. Together they are fondly referred to as The Spectacles. Follow the rock cairns. There is one short scramble section where use of hands may be necessary on the Primitive Trail.

Directions to Trailhead
From Arches Entrance Station, drive 9.0 miles to the signed turnoff to Windows Section. Drive this road another 2.5 miles to the parking area. Spaces for small RVs. Facilities: Pit toilets, recycle bins, no water.

Trail Description
We begin this hike on the main trail and finish on the Primitive Loop which is about 50 feet to the north of the main trail. Both are clearly signed. We visit North Window first ❸, than Turret Arch ❺, than South Window ❻ and on around the loop. If not going around the primitive loop, visit North and South Windows then go to Turret Arch and return to the parking lot from there.

3b: Windows Primitive Loop

Total Distance	1.10 mile loop includes all arches
Difficulty Rating	Easy to Moderate with one very high rock step up on the primitive loop
Surface	Packed gravel, sand, and slickrock
Gradient	Easy to Moderate
Average Time	1 hour
Elevations	TH: 5,146; Gain: +294

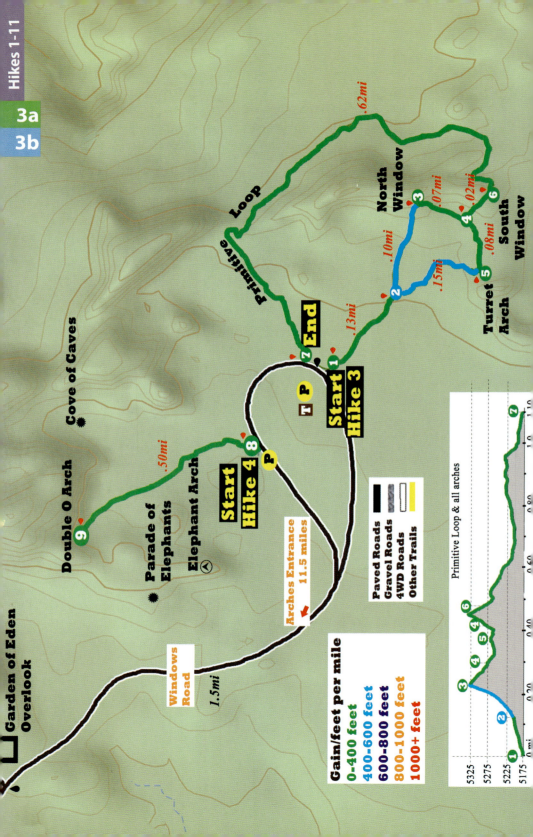

Turret Arch

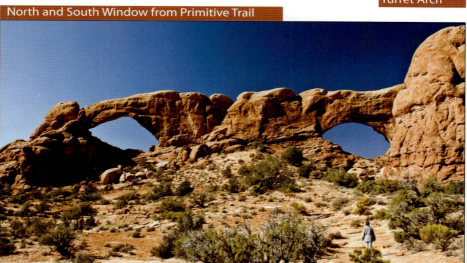

North and South Window from Primitive Trail

GPS	Mile	Elevation	Comment
1	0.00	5,146'	Start Windows Primitive Loop.
2	0.13	5,171'	Signed junction to Turret and South Window. Go straight ahead to North Window.
3	0.23	5,245'	North Window
4	0.30	5,204'	Signed junction: to Turret and South Window. Decide here if going around loop or returning to parking lot.
5	0.38	5,235'	Turret Arch: Go right back to parking lot or go back to ④ to continue on Primitive loop.
4	0.46	5,204'	Back at junction. Turn right to continue to Primitive Loop.
6	0.48	5,217'	South Window. Primitive Trail begins here. Follow the rock cairns.
7	1.10	5,166'	End Primitive Trail at parking lot.

Hikes 1-11

3a
3b

Windows Loops

Double Arch

Double Arch soars above the hikers.

4 Double Arch

Summary

See map on page 40. This is a very short and easy walk through sandy soil to the magnificent Double Arch. From the parking area, you cannot see the second arch. The closer you walk, the more imposing are the arches, formed from a single pothole. Many visitors extend the hike by walking up under the arches. The surrounding area is a fascinating labyrinth of caves and statuettes of stone.

Directions to Trailhead

From Arches Entrance Station, drive 9.0 miles to the signed turnoff to Windows Section. Drive this road another 2.5 miles to the parking area. Parking spaces for small RVs. Facilities: Pit toilets, recycle bins at the upper parking lot. Continue around to "additional parking" for Double Arch Trail.

GPS	Mile	Elevation	Comment
8	0.00	5,095'	Start Double Arch Trail.
9	0.50	5,158'	Return.

Total Distance	1.0 mile RT
Difficulty Rating	Easy
Surface	Sand
Gradient	Easy
Average Time	30 minutes
Elevations	TH: 5,095; Gain: +41
Maps	Trails Illustrated #211 Arches National Park; USGS Arches National Park

Panorama Point Overlook

Views of Arches Park all the way around. Fiery Furnace area, the La Sal Mountains, and the Salt Valley unite for an expansive vista of natural surroundings. Parking lot with spaces for RVs. No facilities. Mile 10.1 from Arches Entrance Station.

Panorama Point Overlook

Delicate Arch

Summary

Delicate Arch stands entirely by itself on a massive sandstone fin. Photographers like to catch a shot of the arch framing the La Sal Mountains in late afternoon and at sunset. The hike itself climbs up a spectacular, long slickrock slope, winds through a small canyon, than hugs a 4 foot wide shelf along a cliff edge before coming around a final, dramatic corner to the arch. No shade. Take water.

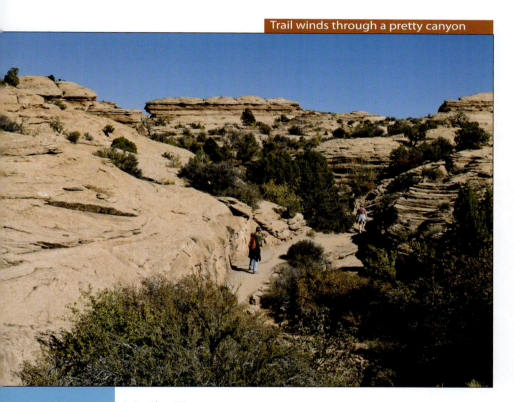

Trail winds through a pretty canyon

Total Distance	3.0 miles RT
Difficulty Rating	Moderate
Surface	Well made packed gravel trail first 0.70 miles; then climb slickrock following cairns. Last section along cliff on 4 foot wide trail.
Gradient	Very Easy on gravel trail; Moderately Steep on slickrock; Moderate to finish
Average Time	3 hours
Elevations	TH: 4,246; Gain: +690 ft
Maps	Trails Illustrated #211 Arches National Park; USGS Arches National Park

Hiking the ledge to the arch

Directions to Trailhead

From Arches Entrance Station, drive Park Road 12.0 miles to signed turnoff for Delicate Arch. Drive another 1.2 miles to parking lot. Facilities: Oversized vehicle parking, pit toilets, trash bins, recycling bins, interpretive signs.

Trail Description

The trail begins at the Wolfe Ranch, an historic pioneer cabin; peek inside and think about what life must have been like for the residents. Cross the Salt Wash on a bridge. Immediately there is a marked junction to a good quality Petroglyph to your left. If you go to the Petroglyph, that trail continues in a short loop back to the main trail. Climb a short, steep hill then walk on the level to the base of the slickrock ❷. Follow rock cairns up the moderately steep slickrock to near the top. Cross a rocky ridge ❸ and enter a small canyon that winds and twists through boulders and sand. The final ascent to the arch follows a rock ledge carved out of the sandstone.

GPS	Mile	Elevation	Comment
1	0.00	4,246'	Start Delicate Arch Trail at Wolfe Ranch parking lot.
2	0.70	4,332'	Gravel trail ends; begin more natural trail.
3	1.10	4,620'	Cross rocky ridge at top of slickrock; enter small canyon.
4	1.50	4,795'	Delicate Arch viewing area.

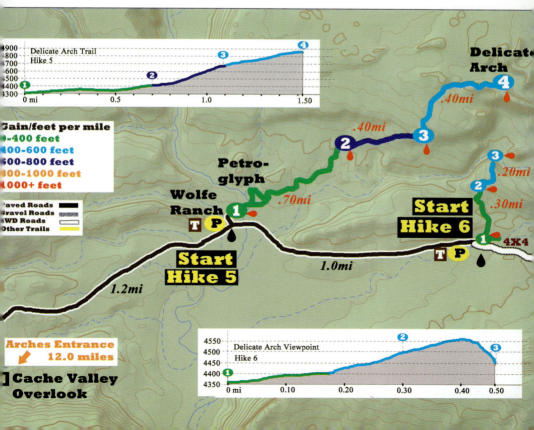

Delicate Arch Viewpoint Trail Options

6a
6b

6a: To Lower Viewpoint

Total Distance	200 yards RT
Difficulty Rating	Easy
Surface	Packed gravel suitable for wheelchairs
Maps	Trails Illustrated #211 Arches National Park; USGS Arches National Park

6b: To Upper Viewpoint

Total Distance	1.0 mile RT
Difficulty Rating	Moderate
Surface	Packed gravel; rock steps, slickrock
Gradient	Moderate
Average Time	45 minutes
Elevations	TH: 4,325; Gain: +325

View from the end of the upper trail

Summary

See map on page 49. There are two viewpoints from this parking area. The first is just a hundred yards on a flat gravel path suitable for wheelchairs. The second viewpoint is a very short hike to a spectacular ridge. The trail climbs moderately steeply up a rocky trail to a first viewpoint, than continues climbing up slickrock marked by rock cairns to the ridge overlooking a deep canyon. Delicate Arch is on the other side of this canyon.

Directions to Trailhead

From Arches Entrance Station, drive 12.0 miles to marked turnoff for Delicate Arch. Drive another 2.2 miles to parking lot (past the parking lot for Delicate Arch Trail). Facilities: Oversized vehicle parking; pit toilets, trash bins, recycling bins, interpretive signs.

Trail Description

From the end of the parking lot, take the right hand trail for the 100 yard viewpoint. Take the left hand trail for the 0.50 mile hike to the ridge viewpoint. This latter trail begins on flat, packed gravel but soon climbs up rocky steps to a viewing area ❷. From there, the trail follows cairns part way up the slickrock ridge. Look for cairns marking a sharp left turn; walk directly towards Delicate Arch which is on the other side of the deep canyon ❸.

GPS	Mile	Elevation	Comment
1	0.00	4,325'	Start Delicate Arch Viewpoint Trail.
2	0.30	4,462'	First viewpoint at top of rocky steps.
3	0.50	4,537'	2nd viewpoint; edge of canyon.

A desert of sand and salt that seems to go on forever. Roadside pull off with space for RVs. No Facilities. Mile 13.6 from Arches Visitor Center.

Salt Valley Overlook

Fiery Furnace Overlook

A 100 yard walk brings visitors to the edge of the Fiery Furnace and views of the La Sal Mountains. Parking lot with tight spaces for even small RVs. Interpretive signs. Pit toilet. Mile 13.8 from Arches Entrance Station.

Fiery Furnace Overlook

Fiery Furnace

Hikes 1-11

7

Guided Tour	
Total Distance	About 2.0 miles RT
Difficulty Rating	Moderately Strenuous
Surface	Some use of hands and scrambling over boulders
Gradient	Moderately Strenuous
Average Time	2 hours
Maps	No trails on any maps

Summary

Fee Area. Fiery Furnace is an area of tall fins created by wind and water. There are narrow slots, and many dead ends like a maze. The name comes from the red glow of the red rocks in the afternoon sunlight rather than from the concept of intense heat. It is actually quite cool in the shaded slots. There are no trails or routes to follow. Hence most visitors go on the ranger guided tour to see this amazing geological labyrinth.

Fiery Furnace guided tour enters this maze

Directions to Trailhead

From Arches Entrance Station, drive north 13.8 miles and turn right (E) into the signed parking lot for Fiery Furnace. Tight parking for even small RVs. Facilities: Pit toilet.

Facts

Reservations must be made well in advance, especially during the high seasons of April, May and October. They cannot be made at the Visitor Center. Make them on the web or by phone:
- National Recreation Reservation Service
- Inside the USA 1-877-444-6777
- Outside the USA: 1-518-885-3639
- On Line: www.Recreation.gov

Be prepared to provide the following information: Location name; desired date, morning or afternoon tour, method of payment and Interagency Senior/Access Pass number if applicable.

Fees are $10.00 for adults; $5.00 for children 5 to 12, and Senior Pass/Golden Age card holders.

If you wish to go on your own, no reservation is necessary but a permit is required. Same fees apply plus you must watch a 15 minute video at the Arches Visitor Center before being allowed to hike there. Remember, there are no marked routes and many dead ends!

Sand Dune Arch Loop Options

Sand Dune Arch

8a: To Sand Dune Arch

Total Distance	0.36 miles RT
Difficulty Rating	Easy
Surface	Deep sand
Gradient	Easy
Average Time	30 minutes
Elevations	TH: 5,127; Gain +124
Maps	Trails Illustrated #211 Arches National Park; USGS Arches National Park

8b: Entire Loop

Total Distance	2.80 mile loop including side trails to Sand Dune Arch & Tapestry Arch
Difficulty Rating	Moderate
Surface	Deep sand, slickrock
Gradient	Easy
Average Time	2 hours
Elevations	TH: 5,127; Gain: +333

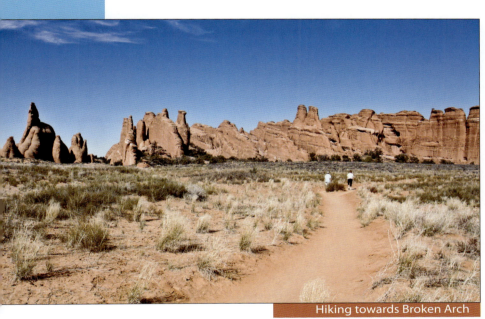

Hiking towards Broken Arch

Summary

The short, easy walk to Sand Dune Arch is extremely popular with families. Once on the trail to Broken Arch and beyond, visitor numbers thin considerably. The loop walk offers a wonderful variety of scenery with minimal effort. Visit three arches; hike a winding route through small canyons and across slickrock; descend on a trail between dramatic fins with towering walls.

Directions to Trailhead

From Arches Entrance Station, drive 15.7 miles to marked parking lot for Broken Arch & Sand Dune Arch TH. Parking lot overflows by mid-morning. Facilities: None.

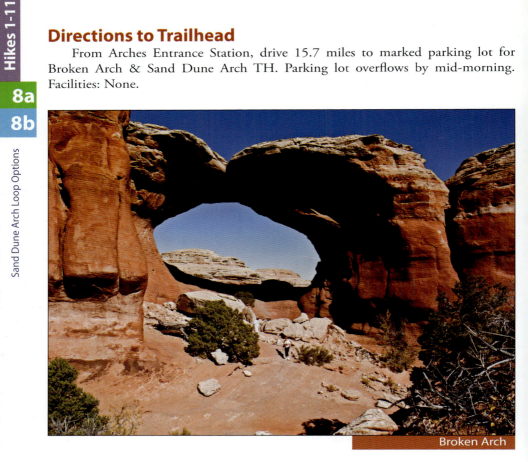

Broken Arch

Trail Description

Come to a marked junction just 0.08 miles from the start ❷. Right goes the short distance to Sand Dune Arch by passing through a narrow gap between massive fins. The arch is tucked away in a corner ❸. Return to the main trail and walk across beautiful grassland with far reaching views of the La Sal Mountains. Another marked junction ❹ leads left to the campground. This is your return route. For now, take the right fork. Broken Arch is visible in the distance. The easy trail begins to wind through boulders until you are at the base of the arch ❺. Climb up the slickrock and walk through the arch. The trail continues on the other side. The trail winds easily through a small canyon, across slickrock, and ascends gradually through deep sand to another marked junction ❻ to Tapestry Arch which you can see in the near distance. This trail dips and winds a bit. Again, climb the slickrock to stand beneath the arch ❼. Two new arches are forming in the same wall. What a treat to see such an amazing process. Return to the main trail and continue to the campground ❽. Turn left on the campground road and walk to site 51 ❾ to pick up the trail back to Sand Dune parking lot. This part of the trail descends through a narrow passage made by massive fins. The towering walls are spectacular. Enjoy! When you exit the narrows, you will be at the junction ❹ and are just a few minutes from the parking lot.

Trail descends through fins after campground.

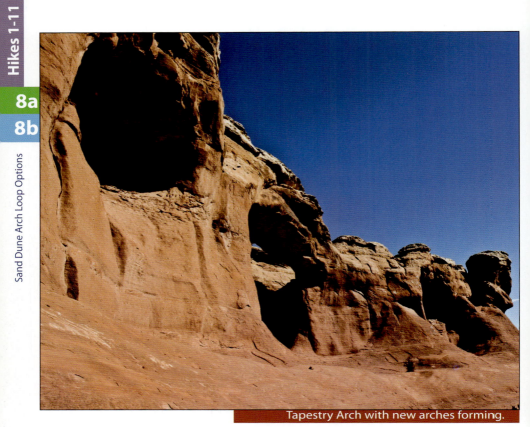

Tapestry Arch with new arches forming.

GPS	Mile	Elevation	Comment
1	0.00	5,127'	Start Sand Dune Loop.
2	0.08	5,119'	Marked junction: go right (S) to Sand Dune Arch; left (N) goes to Broken Arch.
3	0.18	5,294'	Sand Dune Arch
2	0.28	5,119'	Back at marked junction: go left (W) to return to parking lot; go right (N) to continue loop.
4	0.61	5,131'	Marked Junction to Campground. For loop take the right fork (NE).
5	0.86	5,114'	Broken Arch. Go through arch to continue loop.
6	1.34	5,118'	Marked junction to Tapestry Arch. Go right(N) for arch; go straight(W) for campground.
7	1.49	5,108'	Tapestry Arch
6	1.64	5,118'	Back at junction for Tapestry Arch. Go right (W) to continue loop.
8	1.81	5,168'	Enter campground. Go left (S) to site 51 to continue loop.
9	1.91	5,130'	Site 51; follow trail sign to Sand Dune Arch.
4	2.39	5,131'	Marked Junction; go right (S) for parking lot.
2	2.72	5,119'	Marked Junction: go straight (W) to parking lot; left (S) goes to Sand Dune Arch.
1	2.80	5,127'	Finish long loop at Sand Dune Arch parking lot.

Skyline Arch

Total Distance	0.50 mile RT
Difficulty Rating	Easy
Surface	Packed sand
Gradient	Easy
Average Time	20 minutes
Elevations	TH: 5,142; Gain: +52
Maps	Trails Illustrated #211 Arches National Park; USGS Arches National Park

Skyline Arch

Summary
See map on page 63. A wonderfully easy trail to a remarkable arch high on top of a butte. The massive blocks of rocks at your feet fell from the arch.

Directions to Trailhead
From Arches Entrance Station, drive 16.4 miles to the signed roadside pull off. Parking space for small RVs. Facilities: None.

GPS	Mile	Elevation	Comment
1	0.00	5,142'	Start Skyline Arch.
2	0.25	5.082'	Skyline Arch high above.

Devil's Garden Options

Landscape Arch

10a: Landscape Arch

Total Distance	3.02 miles RT includes visiting Tunnel & Pine Tree Arches
Difficulty Rating	Easy
Surface	Good wide gravel packed path
Gradient	Easy but undulating
Average Time	1.5 hours
Elevations	TH: 5,236; Gain: +260
Maps	Trails Illustrated #211 Arches National Park; USGS Arches National Park

10b: Double O Arch

Total Distance	5.90 miles RT which includes visiting all the arches on route
Difficulty Rating	Moderately Strenuous
Surface	Slickrock, deep sand, cliff edges
Gradient	Easy but many short stretches of Moderately Steep elevation changes
Average Time	3.5 hours
Elevations	TH: 5,236; Gain: +1552

10c: Primitive Loop

Total Distance	6.69 miles which includes side trips to all arches except Dark Angel Arch
Difficulty Rating	Moderately Strenuous
Surface	Slickrock, soft sand, and some rocky areas
Gradient	Easy but with many short stretches of Steep slickrock elevation changes
Average Time	4.5 hours
Elevations	TH: 5,236; Gain: +1507

Summary

There are so many amazing sights it is hard to list them all. The arches themselves are wonderful, but the scenery in between is filled with dramatic geological features: Whale fins, spires, towers, massive buttes, expansive vistas with La Sal Mountains for a backdrop. Wildflowers are prolific in season.

Directions to Trailhead

From Arches Entrance gate, drive 17.4 miles on the main road to its end at the signed trailhead. Parking lot fills most mornings. Facilities: Pit toilets, water, trash bins.

Trail Description

Pick your destination based on the options above. Though in summary the trail is colored green for Easy,

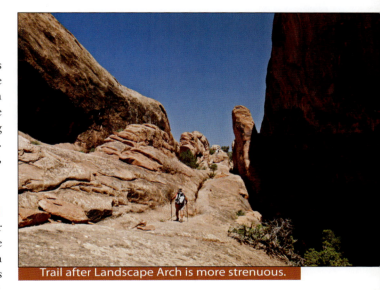
Trail after Landscape Arch is more strenuous.

there are a lot of undulations; some of them are steep. The trail is not flat. From the Start to Landscape Arch ❻, the trail is wide with hard packed gravel creating an easy path for the millions of visitors who want to go only that far. Still, there are plenty of ups and downs in that section alone. If you visit both Tunnel ❸ and Pine Tree ❹ Arches along the way, which have easy access and are very picturesque, you will reach Landscape Arch in 1.51 miles. Landscape Arch spans 306 feet. It is slender thin and continues to lose rock to the forces of nature. To continue on to Double O Arch ❿, the trail undulates even more and sometimes the sand is deep and the trail is rocky. There is slickrock to climb up, narrow, exposed ledges to negotiate. From Double O onward, all the way around the primitive trail back to the parking lot, the trail gradient is still Easy, but there are sections that may necessitate sliding

Crossing the fins on route to Double O Arch.

down your butt on slickrock and there are exposed ledges. You will lose most of the crowds in this section. We recommend doing the loop clockwise. We think it is easier to go down the tricky spots rather than up them.

From Landscape Arch ❻, head towards Double O Arch where the trail immediately becomes rugged as you scramble up a steeper spine of slickrock. Look up and down for great photos. When the trail stops climbing, you will be at the junction for Partition & Navajo Arches ❼. Partition Arch is spectacular ❽. Carved from the belly of a massive fin, (a geological wonder in this park) the hole frames a panoramic vista of tumbled rock, buttes and grasslands beyond. A smaller arch is forming to the right of the big one. Navajo Arch is reclusive, almost hidden in a grotto ❾. You can walk under it, but it is difficult to get far enough away for a full view. These side trips will take some effort as the sand is a bit deep. By the time you get back to the junction, you will have done 2.75 miles.

It is 0.9 mile further on to Double O Arch ❿. About halfway, a viewpoint overlooks the entire heart of Devils Garden: the Fins. This geological phenomenon looks like a pod of whales swimming side by side, with only their massive fins exposed. Then the trail takes you across the top of one of these fins. It is a narrow path with steep cliffs for its edges. We have, in a strong wind, crossed on our hands and knees.

In comparison to the trail, the Double O Arch is less exhilarating as it is difficult to see the stacked arches in one vista. But the trail that got you here was the real prize. You have now hiked 3.65 miles.

The side trip to Dark Angel adds 0.79 miles out & back. By this time you might be dragging from the heat. If you need to make an energy choice, we recommend continuing around the primitive trail and skipping Dark Angel. The Primitive trail is tiring due to deep sand but it is far more spectacular.

From Double O Arch, the primitive trail descends into a wash. The rock formations become more jumbled, carved into fantastic shapes by wind and water. Soon you are scrambling up and down, in and out between the giant fins you viewed from above. Parts of the slickrock trail are too steep to walk. Rocks are worn smooth by bums sliding cautiously downward to the next level. Take your time to enjoy. There are lots of photo opportunities.

Now it is a hard grind back to ❺ as the trail turns to deep sand and climbs steadily for one mile. Keep looking behind and watch the fins change their appearance with elevation. Then, suddenly, the La Sal Mountains, framed by lone, strangely shaped sandstone spires, come into your forward view. Wildflowers bloom across the open expanse. It is simply breathtaking.

By the time you get back to the start, if you went to every arch on every side trip, you would have hiked 6.69 miles. Now it's beer time!

Descending slickrock on primitive loop.

Partition Arch

GPS	Mile	Elevation	Comment
1	0.00	5,236'	Start Devil's Garden Trail.
2	0.26	5,201'	Signed junction: Go right for Tunnel and Pine Tree Arches. Landscape Arch is straight ahead.
3	0.38	5,099'	Tunnel Arch
4	0.58	5,142'	Pine Tree Arch
2	0.78	5,201'	Back at junction; Go right for Landscape Arch; left back to parking lot.
5	1.31	5,185'	Signed junction: Return loop route is the right fork: Take the left fork now.
6	1.51	5,190'	Landscape Arch
7	1.87	5,395'	Signed junction for Navajo & Partition Arches
8	2.09	5,451'	Partition Arch
9	2.50	5,392'	Navajo Arch
7	2.75	5,395'	Back at signed junction for Navajo & Partition Arches
10	3.65	5,387'	Double O Arch
5	5.90	5,190'	Signed junction: Meet trail back to parking lot.
1	6.69	5,236'	Finish Devil's Garden Loop.

Tower Arch Primitive Trail

Total Distance	2.66 miles RT
Difficulty Rating	Moderate
Surface	Very rocky scrambling/hiking at beginning; deep sand, slickrock ledges
Gradient	Moderate with two steeper sections
Average Time	2 hours
Elevations	TH: 5,053; Gain: +723
Maps	Trails Illustrated #211 Arches National Park; USGS Arches National Park

View from top of the first climb.

Summary

Even on a crowded day in Arches, few hikers venture out to this TH. The trail winds and twists through the Klondike Bluffs. There are many varied vistas including big basins encircled by fascinating statuary rock formations; lone pinnacles rising like sentinels; and small, intimate coves bordered by jumbled rocks and fins. Tower Arch is magnificent. This hike will stimulate your interest with scenic wonders from start to finish.

Hikes 1-11

11 — Tower Arch Primitive Trail

Latter section of trail climbs through deep sand.

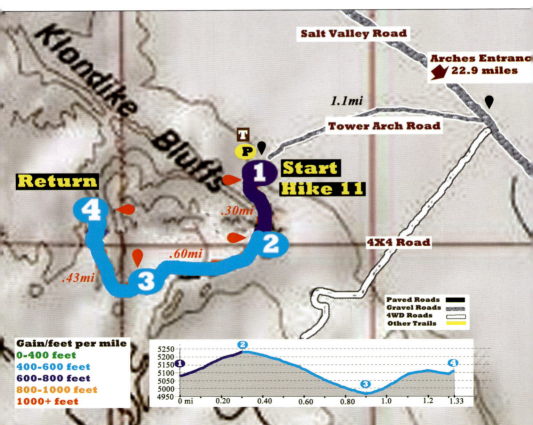

Directions to Trailhead

From Arches Entrance Station, drive 16.1 miles into the park. Just after passing Sand Dune Arch, look for an unmarked gravel road that takes a hard left turn. This is the Salt Valley Road. If conditions are impassable, the gate will be closed. Drive 7.2 miles to a 3-way fork in the road. Do not go straight ahead. Take the middle fork another 1.1 miles to the signed Trailhead. (The left fork is a rough 4x4 road leading into Klondike Bluffs.) Facilities: Pit Toilet, picnic tables, trash.

Trail Description:

The trail begins with a serious climb up slickrock steps and jumbled rocks that require some tricky maneuvering. Once on top of the bluff, ❷, it becomes an easy descending trail over slickrock ledges into a large basin framed by picturesque rock towers ❸. Climb once again up a deep sandy trail and wind into a smaller basin. Tower Arch is well hidden from view until the very end ❹.

GPS	Mile	Elevation	Comment
1	0.00	5,053'	Start Klondike Bluffs Trail.
2	0.30	5,242'	Highest point. Views of Klondike Basin.
3	0.90	4,958'	Low point. Begin ascent through deep sand.
4	1.33	5,044'	Tower Arch

Tower Arch

Island in the Sky
Canyonlands National Park

Island in the Sky is 10.7 miles north of Moab Visitor Center on Hwy 191 and 25 miles west on SR 313. It is truly an island, carved out by the Colorado River and the Green River which meet at about 2200 feet below Grand View Point. Much of the island is flat and grassy with a sprinkling of buttes showing prominently against the forever horizon. It is an easy park to navigate; there are two roads: Grandview Point Road and Upheaval Dome Road with a short spur road to the Green River Overlook and Willow Flat campground. It is 12 miles from the ISVC to the end at Grandview Point. With numerous overlooks to visit, just driving the park is a pleasure.

The magic is at the perimeter where jagged cliffs of red sandstone and white limestone plummet about 1000 feet down to a wide apron that circles the entire island. This apron, called the White Rim, hosts a rugged one hundred mile long 4x4 road that is the favorite of cyclists and 4-wheelers from around the world. It is about another 1200 feet from the White Rim down to the Colorado and Green Rivers. Island in the Sky is a feast of grand vistas and twisting canyons.

Due to such extreme topography, five of the fifteen hikes dive off the cliffs and descend to the White Rim.

They are challenging and spectacular; each offers a totally different experience and view from the others. The shortest descent is from Gooseberry at 5.40 miles round trip; the longest is Wilhite at 11.64 miles round trip. But don't let these distances

Overlooking the route down Gooseberry Trail

The White Rim forms an apron around Island in the Sky Mesa

or difficulty levels deter you from experiencing these amazing trails. Hike to the edge, or descend just part way and return; you will be thrilled by what you see and experience. We even detail practical shorter options for these longer trails to encourage your exploration.

- **Hike 14:** Lathrop has a 5.26 mile RT easy option to the edge of the cliffs.
- **Hike 17:** Wilhite has a 2.56 mile RT easy option to the edge of the cliffs.
- **Hike 18:** Alcove Spring descends almost immediately off the mesa but a short exploration to the Alcove Amphitheater is a moderately strenuous 1.0 miles RT.
- **Hike 22:** Murphy Hogback has an easy 2.0 mile RT to the edge of the cliffs.
- **Hike 24:** Gooseberry goes a mile out to the cliff edge or take the 1.5 mile RT easy trail to the spectacular White Rim Overlook (Hike 25) for an alternative.

Nine hikes are on the mesa top. They lead to wondrous overlooks or explore the buttes and geological features of the Island in the Sky Mesa. They are easy to moderate in distance and difficulty. They are by far the most popular, and therefore more populated, trails in the park.

• **Hike 12:** The Neck winds into intimate canyons and through a variety of high desert habitats. It is the longest trail on the mesa at 5.80 miles and abounds with spring wildflowers.

• **Hike 13:** Shafer Viewpoint Trail is very short, very easy with very spectacular vistas.

• **Hike 15:** Mesa Arch is a popular loop trail to a fabulous arch with a view.

• **Hike 16:** Aztec Butte offers a bit of Aztec history with a granary high atop a butte.

• **Hike 19:** Whale Rock is a fun hike on lots of slickrock.

• **Hike 21:** Upheaval Dome Overlook offers a thrilling view into a massive crater.

• **Hike 23:** Murphy Viewpoint is an easy trail out a promontory overlooking the White Rim.

• **Hike 25:** White Rim Overlook & Trail is another easy trail overlooking a different side of the island. Picturesque cliff edges make wonderful photos.

• **Hike 26:** Grand View Point Overlook & Trail is still another easy hike on a wide, safe trail with plunging cliffs and expansive vistas along the entire route.

Saving the most amazing for last, **Hike 20**, Syncline Loop offers the most variety in scenic wonders. An 8.5 mile loop, it explores the canyons that surround Upheaval Dome Crater and offers a trail that actually enters the Dome area. It is remote, adventurous and strenuous: a winning combination!

The Island in the Sky Visitor Center offers a 15 minute film about the park and is well stocked with books, maps and suggestions for the day including a brochure of ideas for visitors short on time. The park rangers and visitor center staff are encyclopedias of information with a smile. Daily ranger programs provide an in depth look into the history and geology of the park. Whether you have one hour, one day, or one week, there is something fascinating to do for casual and serious hikers/visitors alike at Island in the Sky Canyonlands National Park.

Island in the Sky TH Map

Alcove Springs Trail

Whale Rock

T **20** Syncline Loop **19**
   21 Upheaval Dome **18**
       Overlook

Upheaval Dome Road

Wilhite Trail

17
4.7 m

Green River Overlook

White Rim Road

Green River

- Paved Roads
- Gravel Roads
- 4WD Roads
- Hiking Trails

Island in the Sky Canyonlands National Park Hiking Trails

Neck Spring Loop Options

12a: To Taylor Canyon Viewpoint/Return 1

Total Distance	4.50 miles RT
Difficulty Rating	Moderate
Surface	Mostly desert soil but with numerous sections of loose rock
Gradient	Constant undulating with many very short but steep ups and downs
Average Time	3 hours
Elevations	TH: 5,776; Gain: +1308
Maps	Trails Illustrated 210: Needles & Island in the Sky National Park Utah

View from mesa top of Neck area

Hikes 12-26

12a
12b

12b: Entire Loop

Total Distance	5.80 mile loop
Difficulty Rating	Moderately Strenuous with one steep, short climb up slickrock
Surface	Mostly desert soil but with numerous sections of loose rock
Gradient	Constant undulating with many very short but steep ups and downs
Average Time	4 hours
Elevations	TH: 5,776; Gain: +1547 ft

View into Taylor Canyon from Return 1

Summary

With lots of ups and downs, this is a great conditioning hike. It is not flat! It twists, winds, climbs and descends into four different, intimate box canyons, goes to the edge of Taylor Canyon, climbs up steep slickrock, and saunters along the mesa top with views in every direction. Pear cactus flowers bloom in mid-May.

Directions to Trailhead

From the Island in the Sky Visitor Center, drive south 0.4 miles to the signed Shafer Canyon Overlook & Neck parking lot on the left. The signed trailhead is on the south end of the parking lot.

Trail Description

We hike the loop counterclockwise, going down into the canyon and ending high on the mesa. At mile 3.46 ⑧, the trail ascends very steep slickrock with difficult footing. There are hikers who may not wish to ascend this section and would turn back. This makes a longer hike of 6.92 miles. Be aware that this exists. Plan how far you want to go out and back if you don't want to climb this more difficult slickrock. Here are some suggestions if you want to avoid it.

- Turn back at the Taylor Canyon Overlook ⑤. for a very nice RT hike of 4.50 miles

Steep climb out

- Hike the trail in reverse any distance before descending the steep slickrock
- Make your choice at the trailhead for either of the above:
  - ➤ To hike the reverse, turn left at the trailhead sign and follow the rock cairns to ⑪ which is (south) of the parking lot. From the overlook fence, look for rock cairns going uphill and climb moderately. Soon the trail will become more pronounced.

View into Shafer Canyon near Shafer Trail Overlook

  - ➤ To follow these directions for the standard route counterclockwise, go right at the trailhead sign and cross the road.
- A final and very nice option is to start hiking at ⑩ where there is pullout parking. Hike any distance out the mesa towards ⑨.

The standard route starts by dropping 180 feet in 0.38 miles on a steep but well constructed path. For the next 1.87 miles the trail twists and turns, climbs and retreats in and out of side canyons until you reach mile 2.25 where there is a fine viewpoint overlooking Taylor Canyon as it feeds off to the east ⑤. Another descent through more open vistas takes you to the lowest point at mile ⑥. Then more ups and downs lead to the base of the difficult climb out over slickrock starting at ⑧. This is the hardest part of the trail and may require use of hands, but only lasts for

0.16 mile. Now, back on the mesa top, fine views of the canyons and distant buttes present themselves. It is easy walking mostly over slickrock. After crossing the park road ⑩, you ascend one more time to the edge of Shafer Canyon and follow the cairns back to the parking lot. This section offers the very best views into Shafer Canyon.

GPS	Mile	Elevation	Comment
1	0.00	5,776'	Start & Finish Neck Spring hike.
2	0.38	5,596'	Bottom of 1st descent
3	0.78	5,649'	Photo opportunity
4	1.44	5,734'	Cross tiny stream
5	2.25	5,595'	Photo/grand view of Taylor Canyon. Option 13a; return1.
6	2.81	5,592'	Lowest Point
7	3.28	5,640'	Stream crossing
8	3.46	5,643'	Start strenuous ascent to rim.
9	3.62	5,884'	Rim
10	4.95	5,964'	Cross highway
11	5.35	5,890'	Shafer Trail Overlook pullout
1	5.80	5,776'	End Neck Spring hike.

Shafer Canyon Viewpoint Trail

Hikers walk out Shafer Viewpoint Trail.

Total Distance	0.02 miles RT
Difficulty Rating	Easy
Maps	Trails Illustrated 210: Needles & Island in the Sky National Park Utah

Summary

See map on page 87. Yes, a trail that is only 0.20 miles long gets its own write up. Just walk out to this point and see why.

Directions to Trailhead

Go to the same parking lot as the Neck Trailhead. From the Island in the Sky Visitor Center, drive south just 0.40 miles and turn left into this dual purpose parking lot. The Shafer Viewpoint Trail starts from 2 locations: along with The Neck Trailhead on the south side and on the east side of the parking lot where all the recycle bins are located. There is no trailhead sign at this latter start point.

Trail Description

Follow the rock cairns and rock steps out to the end of the promontory Don't forget your camera. The splendor of Canyonlands is right in front of you! Our cover photo is taken here.

View towards end of trail into Shafer Canyon.

Shafer road descends the cliffs.

Lathrop Options

Hikes 12-26

14a
14b
14c

Canyon rim overlook

14a: To Overlook/Return 1

Total Distance	4.30 miles RT
Difficulty Rating	Easy
Surface	Hard packed sand
Gradient	Easy
Average Time	2.5 hours
Elevations	TH: 6,008; Gain: +359
Maps	Trails Illustrated 210: Needles & Island in the Sky National Park Utah

14b: To Top of Steep Descent/Return 2

Total Distance	6.0 miles RT
Difficulty Rating	Moderate
Surface	Hard packed sand; slickrock ledges
Gradient	Easy to Moderate
Average Time	4 hours
Elevations	TH: 6,008; Gain: + 1644

14c: To White Rim Road/Return 3

Total Distance	10.50 miles RT
Difficulty Rating	Very Strenuous
Surface	Hard packed sand across the top; high steps down on much of the big descent
Gradient	Ranges from Easy to Very Steep
Average Time	8 hours
Elevations	TH: 6,008; Gain: +2849

Summary

Hike an easy trail through pretty grasslands to the edge of a superb lookout, or hike to the White Rim Road on a physically challenging descent and subsequent ascent unless you have left a vehicle on the White Rim Road for a shuttle.

Directions to Trailhead

From Island in the Sky Visitor Center, drive south on the main road 1.9 miles to the signed pull off parking area for Lathrop. Facilities: None. If you set up a shuttle vehicle instead of hiking back up, drive north from the Island in the Sky Visitor Center 0.9 miles and turn right (E) onto the signed Shafer Road. This is a serious 4x4 road with high cliffs and tight switchbacks. It is about 16 miles to the Lathrop TH near Airport Tower Camp. It takes about 2 hours one way.

Hiking along the ledges

Trail Description

Remember, the elevation gained on hiking any trail must include all the ups and downs for the entire journey to be more accurate. This trail has a significant number of big ups and downs to increase a straight mathematical elevation drop of 1662 feet to 2125 feet just to get to the bottom. If you climb back

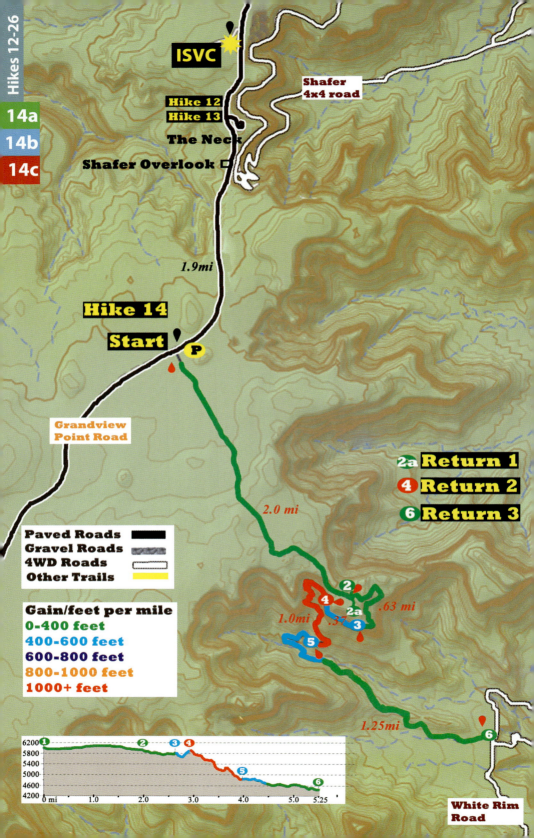

up, the total elevation gain comes to 2849 feet. From the start, hike across open grasslands observing numerous interesting rock formations. About two miles out, there is an unmarked junction in the trail that is quite obvious ❷. Right goes .15 miles out to the viewpoint ❷ₐ which is Return 1 and makes a very nice, easy hike. Go back to the main trail and turn right to continue the hike. The trail descends gently while following several amazing ledges with wonderful views. At ❸, the trail makes a noticeable descent before climbing right back up again to ❹. Between ❸

Looking back at Lathrop Canyon from the White Rim

and ❹ is our favorite section of this hike. It offers many varied views of the canyon below as it contours around many small fingers out and back. If you hike this far, you will have seen the best views of the entire trail. Return 2 is at ❹, before making the long descent to the White Rim. The switchbacks are long and winding; the difficulty is deceiving as many high steps down can be tiring. It took us 4 hours from the TH just to descend to the White Rim Road ❻. The high steps made the ascent back up even more strenuous and time consuming. On a hot afternoon, this is a real workout! Still, the entire trail down to the White Rim has wonderful vistas; it is worth going all the way. That's why we give you the shuttle information!

GPS	Mile	Elevation	Comment
1	0.00	6,008'	Start Lathrop Trail.
2	2.00	5,993'	Unmarked junction: right goes to a viewpoint just .15 miles out. This is Return 1. Left is the main trail.
3	2.63	5,843'	First steep descent that climbs back up again
4	3.00	5,889'	Start second steep descent of 1.0 miles. Return 2.
5	4.00	4,797'	Bottom of second steep descent
6	5.25	4,340'	Trail meets White Rim Road. Return 3 or shuttle.

Mesa Arch Loop

15

Mesa Arch

Total Distance	0.65 mile loop
Difficulty Rating	Easy
Surface	Some broken rock
Gradient	Easy
Average Time	35 minutes
Elevations	TH: 6,113; Gain: +115
Maps	Trails Illustrated 210: Needles & Island in the Sky National Park Utah

Summary

This is a popular, easy loop walk to a fabulous arch that is featured in many photographs. Capture the La Sal Mountains framed inside the arch. Photos face east so best in the afternoon light. Interpretive signs along the route point out a variety of plants. There are steep cliffs just beyond the arch and no fencing.

Directions to Trailhead

From Island in the Sky Visitor Center, drive south 5.9 miles to the signed parking lot for Mesa Arch. Facilities: Pit toilet, recycle bins.

Trail Description

The trail forks left and right at the trailhead. The left fork climbs just a bit less than the right. The trail is well maintained and meanders through gullies and juniper to the arch and back.

GPS	Mile	Elevation	Comment
1	0.00	6,113'	Start Mesa Arch Trail. Left fork is less undulating than the right fork. They make a loop.
2	0.30	6,096'	Mesa Arch
3	0.65	6,113'	End loop

On the trail approaching Mesa Arch

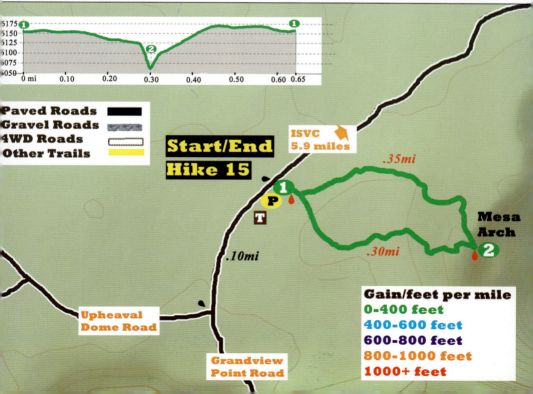

Green River Overlook

Great views of the White Rim

Aztec Butte Options

Hikes 12-26

16a
16b

16a: To First Butte

Total Distance	0.95 mile RT
Difficulty Rating	Easy but with one scramble up a ledge
Surface	Sand and slickrock
Gradient	Easy except for one scramble up a ledge
Average Time	45 minutes
Elevations	TH: 6,064; Gain: +134
Maps	Trails Illustrated 210: Needles & Island in the Sky National Park Utah

Aztec Butte and the slickrock approach

16b: To Aztec Butte

Total Distance	1.61 miles RT
Difficulty Rating	Moderate but a section requires scrambling up very steep slickrock
Surface	Sand and slickrock
Gradient	Mostly easy but with some bouldering up very steep sections; use of hands; exposed ledges
Average Time	1.5 hours
Elevations	TH: 6,064; Gain: +348

Easier slickrock section near the base of Aztec Butte

Summary

Hike to one or both buttes. The first is easy except for one spot where you need to scramble up a short ledge. The Aztec Butte is much more difficult with numerous sections that are very steep slickrock with no real footholds. The best views are from Aztec Mesa where you look straight down Taylor Canyon.

Aztec granary

Some ledge scrambling necessary to get to the top of Aztec Butte

Directions to Trailhead

From the Island in the Sky Visitor Center, drive 6.0 miles to the junction of Grand View Road and Upheaval Dome Road. Turn right (W) on Upheaval Dome Road and drive another 0.7 miles to a signed parking lot for Aztec Butte. No facilities.

Trail Description

There are actually two butte tops to visit. The first junction at ❷ is marked by a rock cairn. Left goes to the easier first butte. Straight ahead goes to Aztec Butte. Our route and profile include hiking to the first butte, returning to the junction at ❷, than hiking to the top of Aztec Butte ❸. The trail to Aztec Butte climbs up the steep slickrock to the very top of the Butte. This deceptively easy looking hike may be too challenging for some folks who have not done any rock scrambling. But you can hike up the easier slick rock and get some fine views without going all the way to the top.

GPS	Mile	Elevation	Comment
1	0.00	6,064'	Start Aztec Butte Trail.
2	0.30	6,069'	Junction marked by cairn. Left goes to first butte.
2	0.65	6,069'	After making the loop on the first butte, return to this point. Go left for Aztec Butte or right to return to parking lot.
4	0.93	6,263'	Aztec Butte granary

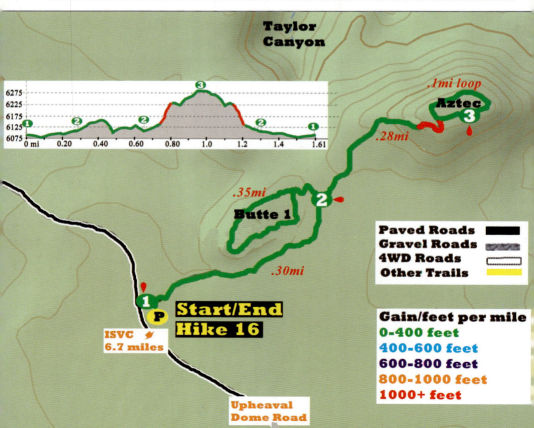

View into Taylor Canyon from Aztec Butte

Wilhite Trail Options

17a: Top of Cliffs/Return 1

Total Distance	2.56 miles RT
Difficulty Rating	Easy
Surface	Mostly sandy soil
Gradient	Easy
Average Time	1.5 hours
Elevations	TH: 5,817; Gain: +408
Maps	Trails Illustrated 210: Needles & Island in the Sky National Park Utah

View into Wilhite Canyon from Return 1

Hikes 12-26

17a
17b
17c

Wilhite Trail Options

17b: Lunch Spot/Return 2

Total Distance	4.98 miles RT
Difficulty Rating	Strenuous
Surface	Loose talus, sand and big rock step downs
Gradient	Very steep descent for 0.86 miles. The rest is easy.
Average Time	3 hours
Elevations	TH: 5,817; Gain: +1621

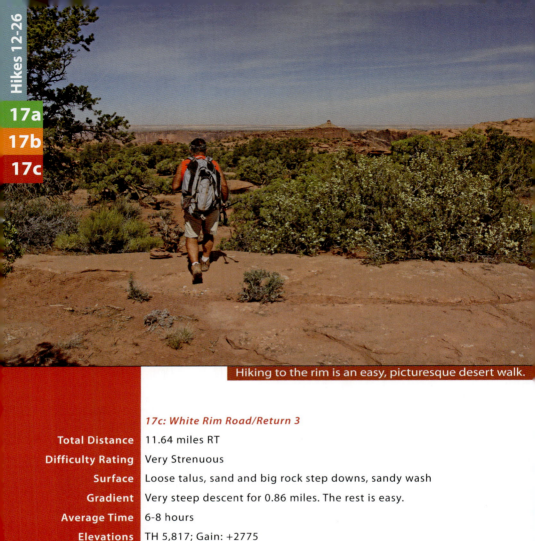

Hiking to the rim is an easy, picturesque desert walk.

17c: White Rim Road/Return 3

Total Distance	11.64 miles RT
Difficulty Rating	Very Strenuous
Surface	Loose talus, sand and big rock step downs, sandy wash
Gradient	Very steep descent for 0.86 miles. The rest is easy.
Average Time	6-8 hours
Elevations	TH 5,817; Gain: +2775

Summary

Take your choice. A picturesque easy walk across the mesa top leads to a spectacular drop off down a very steep canyon wall. It's an amazing spot to contemplate the forces of nature. Continue down this difficult trail that requires some use of hands. Turn around at the bottom of this challenging descent or continue walking out the flat mesa as far as you wish. From this point onward, there are expansive vistas of the White Rim with its buttes and canyons.

Directions to Trailhead

From the Island in the Sky Visitor Center, drive 6.0 miles to the junction of Grand View Point Road and Upheaval Dome Road. Turn right (W) on Upheaval Dome Road and drive 2.0 miles to a wide spot in the road and a small TH sign. No facilities.

Big steps down and back up

Trail Description

This is a difficult descent from the Island in the Sky. Though the steep part is only 0.68 miles, numerous landslides of giant boulders in the path contribute to the difficulty. It is as slow going down as back up. The first 1.28 miles from the parking area however are a delightful hike through varied terrain across the mesa and would make a wonderful easy hike by itself. The flowers are in full bloom by mid-May. You could go as far as the steep descent ❷ and marvel where the trail continues.

If you do continue, once at the bottom of the steep descent ❸, the trail flows out onto a mesa, which is an ideal spot for lunch with a view ❹. The trail stays along the mesa edge for about a half mile more before making another short but steep drop at ❺ through a landslide area to the wash. Once in the wash, there are fewer vistas as the walls of the wash get higher on the descent. We marked three washes (❻-❽) that join the wash you are hiking. You don't want to make a mistake on the return trip and walk up the wrong one! There are good cairn markers along most of the trail.

Lunch spot at Return 2

GPS	Mile	Elevation	Comment
1	0.00	5,817'	Start Wilhite hike.
2	1.28	5,665'	Return 1. Start strenuous descent.
3	2.14	4,833'	End strenuous descent.
4	2.49	4,790'	Return 2. Great lunch spot on Mesa with views of White Rim.
5	3.05	4,832'	Drop into wash for remainder of hike.
6	4.08	4,387'	Big wash comes in from the right (N).
7	4.21	4,371'	Little wash comes in from the left (S).
8	5.08	4,266'	Another little wash from the left (S)
9	5.82	4,185'	Return 3. Trail meets White Rim Road.

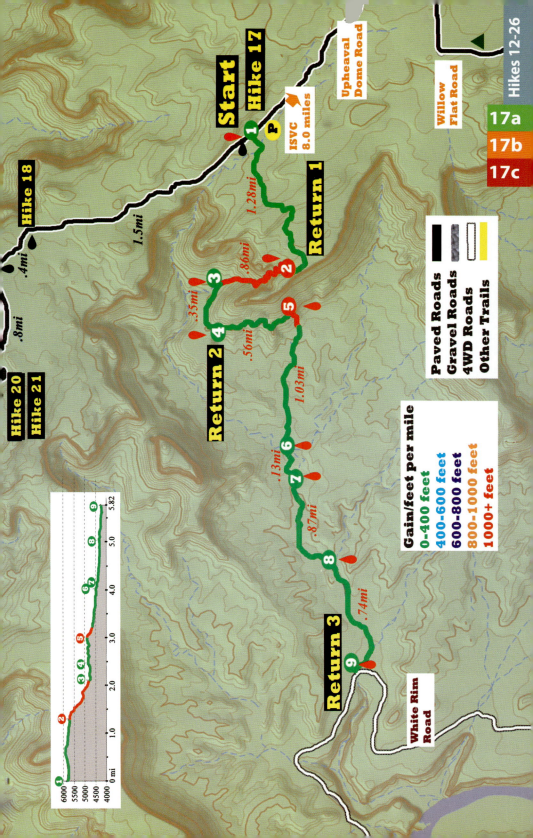

Alcove Spring Options

Hikes 12-26

18a
18b

View from edge into canyon

18a: To Alcove Amphitheater/Return 1

Total Distance	2.0 miles RT
Difficulty Rating	Moderately Strenuous
Surface	Steep descent is mixture of slickrock and trail; wash is compacted soil.
Gradient	Very Steep
Average Time	1.5 hours
Elevations	TH: 5,677; Gain: +875
Maps	Trails Illustrated 210: Needles & Island in the Sky National Park Utah

18b: To Taylor Canyon Road/Return 2

Total Distance	11.0 miles RT
Difficulty Rating	Strenuous
Surface	Steep descent is mixture of slickrock and trail; wash is compacted soil.
Gradient	Very Steep first mile than very Easy
Average Time	7 hours
Elevations	TH: 5,677; Gain: +2104

Summary

Drop instantly and very steeply off the mesa and hike through a wide canyon to visit Moses & Zeus a spectacular rock formation. Overall, this is the least strenuous/difficult of the hikes to the White Rim.

Directions to Trailhead

From the Island in the Sky Visitor Center, drive 6.0 miles to the junction of Grand View Point Road

Hiking the lovely canyon bottom

and Upheaval Dome Road. Turn right (W) on Upheaval Dome Road and drive another 3.5 miles to the signed parking area for Alcove Spring. Facilities: None.

Alcove Spring

Moses & Zeus

Trail Description

Drop off the mesa almost immediately into the very picturesque Trail Canyon. The route down the steep section has been compromised by Mother Nature over the years with a few detours around slides and rock cairns that have disappeared. It is not like Murphy Hogback with the well maintained, carved steps. It is one mile of steep, losing about 1127 feet. It is another 1.33 miles of easy gradient to the wash which makes a good return point for a shorter hike ❷. After that, the trail descends 516 feet in 3.17 miles to the intersection with Taylor Canyon Road ❸. Spectacular views of Moses and Zeus rock formations make this junction our second return point. It is about another 0.25 miles to the backcountry campsite.

GPS	Mile	Elevation	Comment
1	0.00	5,677'	Start Alcove Spring Trail.
2	2.33	4,409'	Return 1: Trail meets wash. Follow wash to Taylor Canyon.
3	5.50	4,239'	Return 2: Meet Taylor Canyon Road. Views of Moses & Zeus.

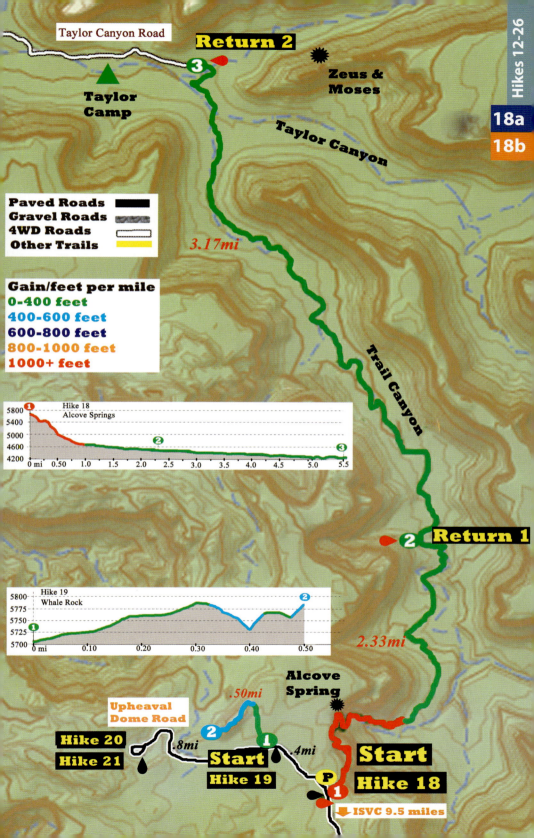

Whale Rock

Total Distance	1.0 miles RT
Difficulty Rating	Moderate
Surface	Climbing up the face of slickrock
Gradient	Moderate
Average Time	40 minutes
Elevations	TH: 5,682; Gain: +223
Maps	Trails Illustrated 210: Needles & Island in the Sky National Park Utah

Summary

See map on page 115. This is a wonderful hike meandering through slick rock buttes and climbing up slickrock to a high point with 360 degree views of Island in the Sky Peninsula.

Directions to Trailhead

From the Island in the Sky Visitor Center, drive 6.0 miles to the junction of Grand View Road and Upheaval Dome Road. Turn right (W) on Upheaval Dome Road and drive another 3.9 miles to the signed parking area for Whale Rock. Facilities: Trash bins.

Hiking out to the whale's head

19

Trail Description

The trail meanders through sandy washes around buttes and mounds until starting a steeper ascent directly up the whale's back. Follow rock cairns for the route. The whale has a "hump" that can be ascended with a little scrambling. Or walk around the hump on the left side and hike up the steep slickrock to the whale's head. There are no handrails as described at the trailhead. The slickrock is steep, but nothing like climbing up the Aztec Butte rock. We rate this hike Moderate only because of the steeper parts of the slickrock.

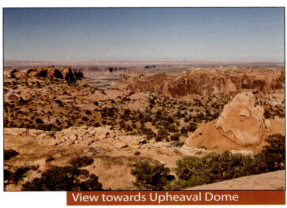

View towards Upheaval Dome

GPS	Mile	Elevation	Comment
1	0.00	5,682'	Start Whale's Rock.
2	0.50	5,810'	Top of whale's head

Syncline Loop

Rough & tumble Syncline Canyon

Total Distance	8.5 mile loop
Difficulty Rating	Very Strenuous
Surface	A great variety including some bouldering around rocks and drops
Gradient	Steep and difficult ascents & descents. Easy through Upheaval Wash.
Average Time	7.5 hours
Elevations	TH: 5,656; Gain: +2949
Maps	Trails Illustrated #210 Needles & Island in the Sky Canyonlands National Park

Summary
Of all the hikes in Canyonlands, this is perhaps the most diverse in scenic wonder. Descend down steep slickrock boulders, hike through massive canyons, meander through long twisting washes, all surrounded by fascinating rock formations.

Hikes 12-26

20

Syncline Loop

Starting the steep descent

Peek-a-boo views of the valley bottom which is still far away

Directions to Trailhead

From the Island in the Sky Visitor Center drive south 6.0 miles to the Upheaval Dome and Grandview junction. Turn right (W) and drive 4.7 miles to the parking lot. Facilities: picnic tables, pit toilets and recycle bins.

Trail Description

This is a difficult trail due to its length (especially if you add the 3.0 mile round trip into the Dome), the steep descents and ascents, and the occasional bouldering needed to get around some obstacles. We hike the trail clockwise because the ascent back up Syncline is more gradual. When you leave the parking lot, follow the signs to Upheaval Dome. In 100 feet, you will encounter a 3 way junction. Straight ahead is the short trail to Upheaval Dome Overlook, a magnificent hike (21) included on the map for this hike. Turn left instead to start the Syncline Loop trail. The first 0.88 miles winds through jumbled boulders but descends insignificantly. When you reach the big descent ❷, the plunge down is obvious. Dropping 1178 feet in one mile, the steps are steep and the trail is filled with scree and loose rock. A crew is currently reconstructing a portion of the trail that used to require sliding down the slickrock on your butt. If you like drama, this is a great place to experience it. The vistas are superb in every direction, the trail is challenging and you may likely be all by yourself. Once you reach the bottom of the descent ❸ the trail follows Upheaval Wash and is easy walking for a while. At ❹ is the junction where Upheaval Canyon Trail takes off left and descends to the White Rim Road. It is a 3.5

Flowers bloom well in the valley bottom.

miles one way option you can take but it requires a long and difficult shuttle on the White Rim Road. Continuing around, you are now in Syncline Wash and starting to ascend. A quick steep climb gets you to ❺ and the junction with the Upheaval Dome Trail. If you are strong and energetic, we recommend this 3 mile round trip. The trail ascends not too steeply into the crater of Upheaval Dome ❺ₐ. Go as far as you wish. You are in the bowels of a volcanic crater. Geologists think the crater was formed by a meteor, or the salt remnants of an ancient ocean buckling under the enormous pressure of miles of silt compressed into rock. Regardless, we recommend hiking the Upheaval Dome Overlook Trail (Hike 21) at some time during your visit to Canyonlands to see this amazing crater close up.

A very picturesque canyon indeed!

Back at the main trail, very soon the serious business of climbing out begins. It is a long haul. The trail enters the narrow Syncline valley, twisting its way up through heavier vegetation. It is obvious more water collects in this valley. There are even water holes ❻ to replenish your supply, but you would need a filter. The most difficult part of the trail requires scrambling and bouldering around massive rocks. Watch closely for cairns. It is easy to lose your way here. At Canyon Junction ❽, go right. Though still steep, the narrow canyon begins to open up. By ❾, the trail eases considerably. There is even some flat! Finally you crest the rim and drop a short distance to your starting point. Congratulations! A well deserved beer is hopefully waiting in your cooler back at the vehicle.

GPS	Mile	Elevation	Comment
1	0.00	5,656'	Start & Finish Syncline Loop.
2	0.88	5,563'	Start steep descent.
3	1.98	4,385'	Bottom of steep descent
4	3.27	4,226'	Junction: Go straight; Left is Upheaval Canyon Trail to White Rim.
5	3.52	4,258'	Junction: Right goes to Upheaval Dome side trip; left continues Syncline Loop.
6	4.49	4,806'	Water hole
7	4.82	4,873'	Cave
8	5.53	4,859'	Canyon Junction : Go right.
9	6.07	5,264'	Trail eases to finish.
1	8.50	5,656'	Finish Syncline Loop

Upheaval Dome Overlook Trail

Upheaval Dome

21a: To First Overlook

Total Distance	0.60 mile RT
Difficulty Rating	Easy
Surface	Rock steps and packed sand
Gradient	Easy
Average Time	45 minutes
Elevations	TH: 5,653; Gain: +158
Maps	Trails Illustrated 210: Needles & Island in the Sky National Park Utah

21b: To Second Overlook

Total Distance	1.60 miles RT
Difficulty Rating	Moderate
Surface	Rock steps, packed sand, slickrock
Gradient	Easy to Moderate
Average Time	1.5 hours
Elevations	TH: 5,653; Gain: +496

Summary

See map on page 123. This is a very popular trail, especially to the first overlook. Upheaval Dome is a geological wonder, thought to have been created by the distillation of thick underlying layers of salt, causing a complete collapse of landforms, or perhaps by a meteorite. Both viewpoints offer stunning perspective on the results.

Directions to Trailhead

From the Island in the Sky Visitor Center drive south 6.0 miles to the Upheaval Dome and Grandview junction. Turn right (W) and drive 4.7 miles to the parking lot. Facilities: picnic tables, pit toilets and recycle bins. This is the same trailhead as Syncline Loop Trail.

Climbing slickrock to second overlook

A well constructed trail near the start

Trail Description

The trailhead leaves the parking lot at the south end. In 100 feet, you will encounter a 3-way junction. Go straight ahead for the short trail to Upheaval Dome. Left and right are the Syncline Loop Trail. The trail climbs a series of rock steps most of the way to the first overlook where there is a wonderful interpretive sign explaining the amazing events that may have created Upheaval Dome. Backtrack down the trail just a bit to go to the second overlook. This trail weaves in and out of small bluffs, descending moderately to the end of the trail at a cliff edge. Wow!

GPS	Mile	Elevation	Comment
1	0.00	5,653'	Start Upheaval Dome Overlook Trail.
2	0.30	5,779'	First Overlook
3	0.80	5,581'	Second Overlook
1	1.60	5,653'	Finish back at parking lot.

Hiking the trail to the second overlook

Murphy Hogback Loop

22a
22b
22c

View from the rim

22a: Murphy Hogback to Cliffs/Return 1

Total Distance	2.0 miles RT
Difficulty Rating	Easy
Surface	Mostly sand
Gradient	Easy
Average Time	1 hour
Elevations	TH: 6,253; Gain: +228
Maps	Trails Illustrated 210: Needles & Island in the Sky National Park Utah

22b: Murphy Hogback to Murphy Camp/Return 2

Total Distance	9.54 miles RT
Difficulty Rating	Strenuous
Surface	Sand, rock stairs
Gradient	Very steep descent for 0.75 miles, Easy after that
Average Time	6.5 hours
Elevations	TH: 6,253; Gain: +2104

22c: Murphy Hogback Loop

Total Distance	10.0 miles Loop
Difficulty Rating	Strenuous
Surface	Slickrock steps, deep sand in wash, road bed, and desert soil
Gradient	Very Steep descent for 0.75 miles, Easy on Hogback Ridge, steep road descent, Easy in wash
Average Time	7 hours
Elevations	TH: 6,253; Gain: +2258

Summary

Amazing vistas from the entire steep section and Hogback Ridge. Hike the entire loop or walk out Hogback Ridge as far as you wish and return the same way. This is the easiest and perhaps the best hike down to the White Rim if considering effort verses views.

Directions to Trailhead

From Island in the Sky Visitor Center, drive 8.2 miles (passing the junction of Grand View Point Road and Upheaval Road) to signed TH parking lot. No Facilities.

Trail Description

This is a well built trail considering the steepness off the rim. It is much less exposed and the steps are easier than the Gooseberry Trail. There are also more level

It's an easy hike to the edge of the rim.

The descent begins. The Hogback ridge is to the far right.

sections within the steep part which is refreshing. The initial mile to the rim is an easy downhill gradient in a sandy wash. A junction ❷ at mile 0.45 marks the trail to Murphy Overlook which is an easy 3.4 mile out & back hike (23). As soon as you start descending at ❸, panoramic views of multiple canyons cutting into the White Rim keep you constant company. At mile 1.86 is the junction where you decide which way to go ❹. If you want to do the entire loop, we recommend going right out the Hogback and returning via the sand wash. The wash is very sandy and slow going. It is also deep enough that there are few views of anything but its walls and some buttes high above. For this reason, you may decide to walk out and back on the Hogback Ridge with its 360 degree panorama to Murphy Camp ❻ and return the same way skipping the wash entirely. If you continue the loop, follow the 4x4 road for 0.96 miles. The road is steep at first, than undulates to a signed junction ❼. Leave the road and start hiking up the sandy wash back to ❹ and the top.

GPS	Mile	Elevation	Comment
1	0.00	6,253'	Start Murphy Hogback hike.
2	0.45	6,141'	Junction to Murphy Overlook
3	1.00	6,063'	Start Steep descent of 757 feet: Return 1
4	1.86	5,206'	Bottom of steep descent. Go right for Hogback Ridge.
5	4.52	5,263'	Junction with White Rim Road. Go left for Murphy Camp.
6	4.77	5,217'	Murphy Camp: Return 2
7	5.73	4,819'	Junction White Rim Road sandy wash
4	8.14	5,206'	Junction: Start steep ascent to return to TH.
3	9.00	6,063'	Top of steep ascent
2	9.55	6,141'	Junction to Murphy Overlook
1	10.00	6,253'	Finish hike.

Murphy Overlook

Hikes 12-26 | 23

Viewpoint with Hogback Trail below

Total Distance	3.40 miles RT
Difficulty Rating	Easy
Surface	Sand and some loose gravel
Gradient	Easy
Average Time	2 hours
Elevations	TH: 6,219; Gain: +292
Maps	Trails Illustrated 210: Needles & Island in the Sky National Park Utah

Summary

See map on page 131. This is a wonderful, easy walk out a long promontory to a grand view of the Murphy Hogback ridge and the White Rim.

Directions to Trailhead

From Island in the Sky Visitor Center, drive 8.2 miles (passing the junction of Grand View Point Road and Upheaval Road) to signed TH parking lot. No Facilities.

Trail heads out a promontory

GPS	Mile	Elevation	Comment
1	0.00	6,219'	Start Murphy Trail.
2	0.45	6,159'	Signed junction: go right for Murphy Overlook. Left goes to Murphy Hogback.
3	1.70	6,056'	Overlook

Trail Description

This is the same trailhead as the Murphy Hogback hike. Walk the flat, easy trail to the signed junction at ❷ and take the right fork. The trail goes down and up a bit from there, and some sections have loose broken rock. Views of the La Sal Range are behind you and views off either side of the promontory are splendid. Best photos of the canyon side are in the morning.

Great views off both sides of the promontory

The White Rim encircles Island in the Sky.

Buck Canyon Overlook

Gooseberry Trail

View from Rim

Total Distance	5.40 miles RT
Difficulty Rating	Moderately Strenuous
Surface	Natural rock and boulders for steep stepping first mile, Easy desert soil after that
Gradient	Very Steep first mile, Easy undulating after that
Average Time	4-6 hours
Elevations	TH: 6,219; Gain: +1457
Maps	Trails Illustrated 210: Needles & Island in the Sky National Park Utah

Summary

Hard to believe there is a trail here at all. It plummets off the rim immediately affording constant incredible views of the White Rim and its deeply carved canyons with the La Sal Mountains for a backdrop. High straight cliffs contain the upper part of the trail to a goat-like descent. When you arrive at the White Rim road, another massive canyon plummets down just yards ahead. Spectacular! This is the shortest route to the White Rim.

Directions to Trailhead

From Island in the Sky Visitor Center, drive south 10.8 miles on the main park road, passing the junction to Upheaval Dome Road. Turn left (E) into the picnic area. The sign does not mention the trailhead. Facilities: picnic tables and pit toilets. No water.

Well made steps help in the descent.

Gooseberries

Hiking the wash. The descent came down through the notch above.

Ascending the steep back to the top

Trail Description

The trail is very easy for the first 0.8 miles to a signed junction at ❷ where the very steep descent begins. Although the total elevation change is only 1457 feet, (making this a Moderately Strenuous hike overall), the 1.17 mile descent is very difficult. The steps are often very high requiring a jump, or sit down approach. Loose talus and very narrow portions along steep cliff edges require attention. There are numerous places where being a goat would be a benefit. There are only a few areas where this part of the trail allows normal walking. After you enter the wash at ❸, it is an easy saunter all the way to the trails end at ❹. The return trip back up took an additional half hour in all. Take plenty of water as you will not find any on route.

GPS	Mile	Elevation	Comment
1	0.00	6,219'	Start Gooseberry hike.
2	0.08	6,217'	Signed junction; go left for Gooseberry; start steep descent.
3	1.25	5,052'	Bottom of steep descent. Enter wash.
4	2.70	4,682'	Junction with White Rim Road. Return.

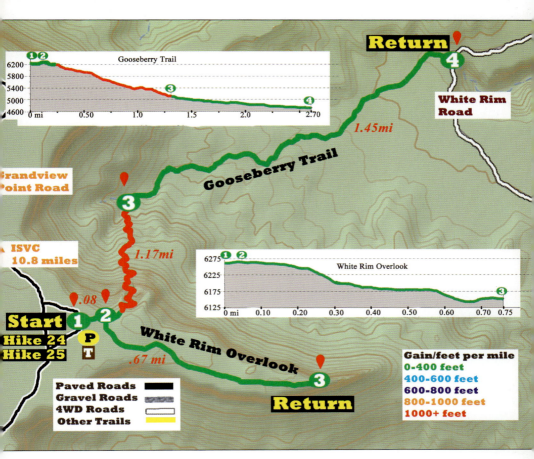

White Rim Overlook Trail

The viewpoint

Total Distance	1.50 miles RT
Difficulty Rating	Easy
Surface	Mostly gravel with a few rock steps
Gradient	Easy
Average Time	1 hour
Elevations	TH: 6,247; Gain: +135
Maps	Trails Illustrated 210: Needles & Island in the Sky National Park Utah

Summary

See map on page 139. This is a very easy short hike. The trail descends very gently, leading out a large promontory to a fabulous view of the White Rim below. Best photos in the afternoon.

Directions to Trailhead

This is the same trailhead as the Gooseberry Trail. From Island in the Sky Visitor Center, drive south 10.8 miles on the main park road, passing the junction to Upheaval Dome Road. Turn left (E) into the picnic area. The sign does not mention the trailhead. Facilities: picnic tables and pit toilets, recycle bins and trash. No water.

An easy trail leads to the wonderful view.

Trail Description

The trail begins mid-way around the parking lot and is well signed. Almost immediately, you come to the signed junction for Gooseberry Trail ❷. Go right here for the Overlook Trail. The trail wanders easily downhill with just a few spots with rocky steps to negotiate. When the trail ends ❸, it is possible to scramble out on various rocks for great photos.

GPS	Mile	Elevation	Comment
1	0.00	6,247'	Start White Rim Overlook Trail.
2	0.08	6,217'	Signed junction: Go right. Left is Gooseberry Trail.
3	0.75	6,062'	Return.

Grandview Point Trail

A grand view indeed!

Total Distance	2.0 miles RT
Difficulty Rating	Easy
Surface	Mostly slickrock
Gradient	Easy
Average Time	1.5 hours
Elevations	TH: 6,279; Gain: +498
Maps	Trails Illustrated 210: Needles & Island in the Sky National Park Utah

Summary

Views, views, views! This hike is short, easy, and packed with vistas of mountain ranges 35 miles away. The White Rim plateau is 1000 feet straight down, and the deep gorges of the Colorado and Green Rivers are 2000 feet below the trail.

Directions to Trailhead

From Island in the Sky Visitor Center, drive south 12.0 miles to the end of the paved road following signs to Grand View Point. Large parking lot with spaces for Rvs; pit toilet, recycle bins, no water.

Trail Description

This is an easy undulating hike with a few sections of carved stone steps to negotiate. There are many places to walk out on the slickrock to the very edge of

Grandview Point Trail

the steep cliffs. Pinion pines, snags, rabbit brush and a scattering of red paint brush dot the landscape. Strong winds can blow on this exposed mesa top.

GPS	Mile	Elevation	Comment
1	0.00	6,279'	Start Grand View Point hike.
2	1.00	6,188'	End of trail. Return.

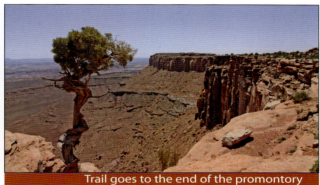

Trail goes to the end of the promontory

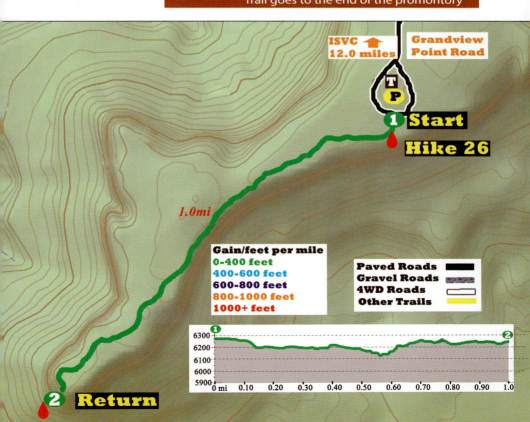

Gain/feet per mile
0-400 feet
400-600 feet
600-800 feet
800-1000 feet
1000+ feet

Paved Roads
Gravel Roads
4WD Roads
Other Trails

Grandview Point Overlook

You don't have to hike the trail to get this view!

Needles Canyonlands National Park

Needles District of Canyonlands National Park is a hiking wonderland. From arches, to stone mushrooms, pillars, towers, slot canyons and keyholes, the trails meander through, around, and over these fascinating red rock formations. Views expand to the La Sal Range, Island in the Sky and west into the Maze. More

The famous Needles as seen from Chesler Trail.

than buttes and towers, Needles offers hikes through lushly vegetated canyons with flowing streams in the spring; enjoy the cottonwoods turning yellow in the fall. There are many hikes for all abilities ranging from 0.60 miles to 10.9 miles and beyond. Because many trails form loops and interconnect, it is possible to create your own route; for this reason, Needles is a very popular backpacking destination.

Needles is a compact park. The paved road through the park is just over six miles long. Four-wheelers enjoy the many backcountry roads, including the most famous and difficult: Elephant Hill.

There are choices for camping both in the park and nearby areas outside the park. See appendix B for more details. Squaw Flats Campground in the park is situated amongst interesting rock formations. Four of the popular hikes we describe begin from this campground.

- **Hike 34:** Peekaboo Springs is a round trip that is well suited for hiking out any distance desired
- **Hike 35:** Squaw Canyon/Big Spring Canyon loops through two of the vegetated canyons and is the easiest trail of the four mentioned here

- **Hike 36:** Big Spring/Elephant Canyon is a more strenuous but spectacular loop over various saddles with big views
- **Hike 37:** Squaw Canyon/Lost Canyon loops with still another vegetated canyon but offers a fascinating climb through a narrow notch and clambers down the other side through ledges and boulders

These trails all connect to four more that start at the Elephant Hill parking lot. Combined together they create an unending possibility of interesting backpacking routes.

- **Hike 38:** Elephant Hill to Squaw Flats CG is intoxicating. A great shorter hike with infinite variety
- **Hike 39:** Druid Arch is a RT trail that ends at a very unusual arch.
- **Hike 40:** Chesler Loop is perhaps the most famous. If you find the 10.3 mile hike too long, go anyway. The entire trail is gorgeous so any distance makes a winner of the day
- **Hike 41:** Devil's Kitchen loops through sections of Chesler while visiting two entirely different areas: a wide grassy basin surrounded by monolithic red walls, and a winding, twisting route through fascinating stone mushrooms

Within the remaining trails, hikers will find the shortest options in the park
- **Hike 27:** Roadside Ruin
- **Hike 28:** Cave Spring
- **Hike 31:** Pothole Point
- **Hike 42:** Squaw Flats Campground Loops A&B

Needles District is about 40 miles south of Moab on Hwy 191. Turn right on Utah 211 (opposite Church Rock) and drive another 34 miles to the park entrance. The junction is signed. Do not turn right at the sign further north that says Needles Overlook. That is a 20 mile road to a fascinating viewpoint, but it does not connect to Needles Park!

The visitor Center is just .30 miles beyond the entrance station and is a fascinating visit all on its own. There are books, maps, displays, films, and of course very helpful personnel eager to answer your questions. A fine backcountry section supplies any necessary permits as well as maps and information.

Welcome to Needles District, Canyonlands National Park!

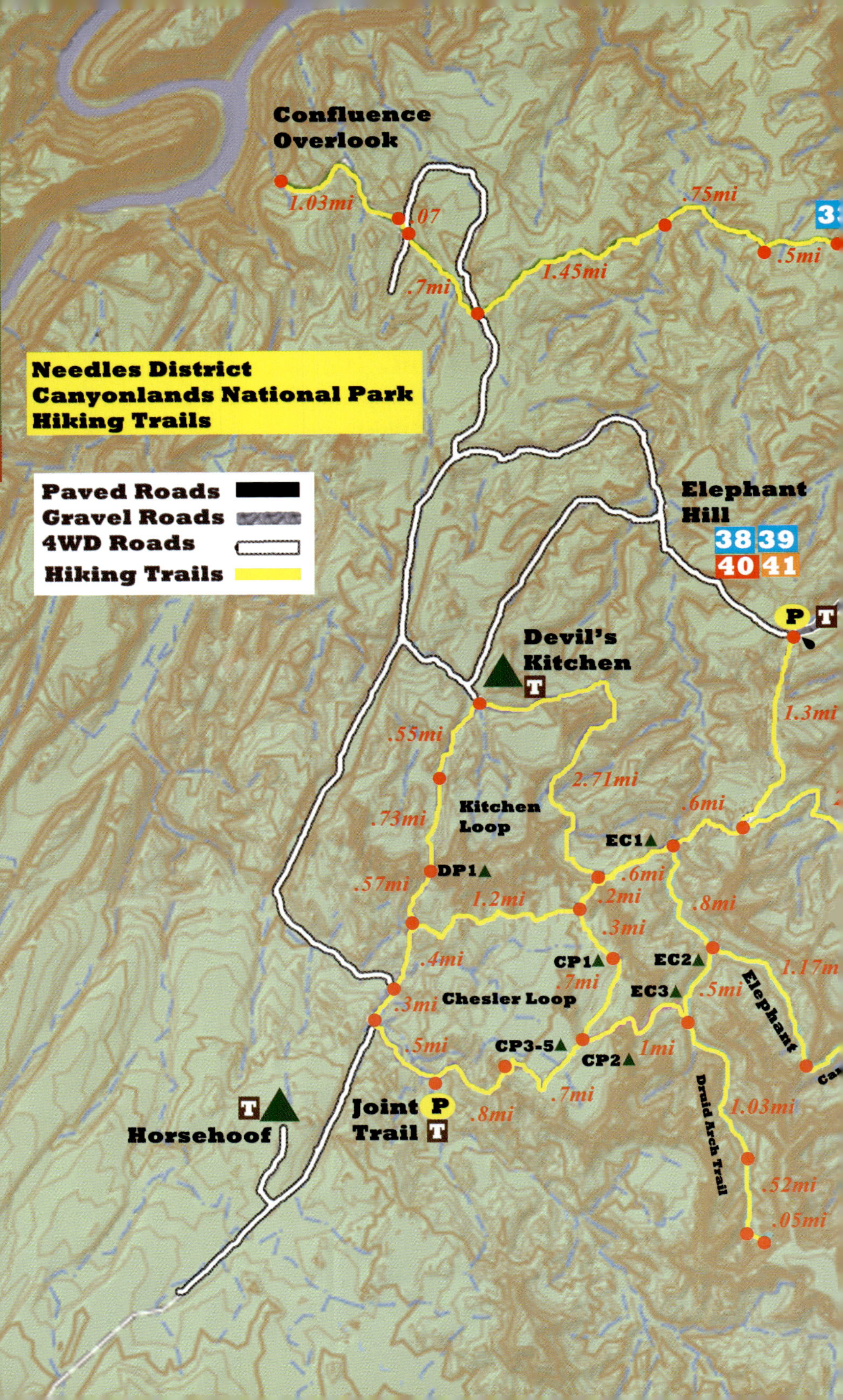

Needles TH Map

Needles District
Canyonlands National Park
Hiking Trails

Legend:
- Paved Roads
- Gravel Roads
- 4WD Roads
- Hiking Trails

Confluence Overlook — 1.03mi, .07, .7mi, 1.45mi, .75mi, .5mi

Elephant Hill — 38 39 40 41, P T, 1.3mi

Devil's Kitchen — .55mi, .73mi, .57mi, 2.71mi, .6mi, .8mi

Kitchen Loop — DP1, 1.2mi, .6mi, .2mi, .3mi, EC1, EC2, EC3, 1.17mi

Chesler Loop — .4mi, .3mi, CP1, .7mi, .5mi, 1mi

Horsehoof — T

Joint Trail — P T, .5mi, CP3-5, CP2, .7mi, .8mi

Druid Arch Trail — 1.03mi, .52mi, .05mi

Elephant Canyon

Roadside Ruin

Hikes 27-42

27

This ruin is in very good condition protected by the overhang.

Total Distance	0.30 mile loop
Difficulty Rating	Easy
Surface	Packed gravel and sand, slickrock
Gradient	Easy
Average Time	20 minutes
Elevations	TH: 4,945; Gain: Insignificant
Maps	Trails Illustrated 210: Needles & Island in the Sky National Park Utah

Hikes 27-42

27

Roadside Ruin

Summary

A short, easy trail goes to a well preserved granary and makes a loop back across slickrock. Pick up a 50 cent brochure at the trailhead that tells about the structure and different plants along the trail and how the Indian society used them.

Directions to Trailhead

From Needles Entrance Station, drive 0.6 miles to the signed parking lot for Roadside Ruin. Facilities: Trash bins.

GPS	Mile	Elevation	Comment
1	0.00	4,945'	Start Roadside Ruin.
2	0.15	4,940'	Granary
1	0.30	4,945'	Finish Loop.

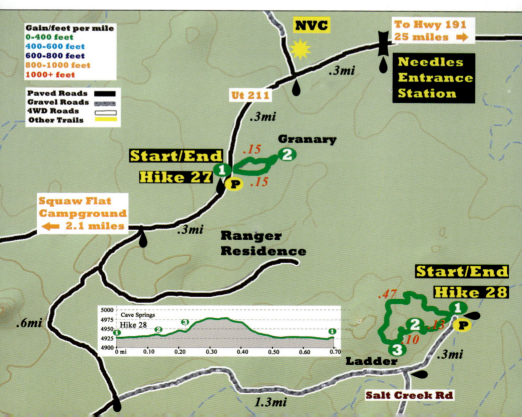

Cave Springs

View from the slickrock section.

Total Distance	0.70 mile loop
Difficulty Rating	Easy
Surface	Sand and slickrock
Gradient	Easy but with 2 ladders to climb
Average Time	30 minutes
Elevations	TH: 4,896; Gain: +72
Maps	Trails Illustrated 210: Needles & Island in the Sky National Park Utah

Summary

See map on pg. 151. This is a wonderful easy trail that winds through an area of interesting caves that display ancient rock art and modern cowboy artifacts. This is a good opportunity for beginner hikers to acquaint themselves with hiking on slickrock and following rock cairns.

Directions to Trailhead

From Needles Entrance Station, drive 0.9 miles to the signed turnoff for Cave Springs and Salt Creek. Drive this paved road 0.6 miles to a T junction. Turn left on the gravel road and drive to the end at mile 1.6. Space for RVs. Facilities: Trash bins.

Trail Description

There are two ladders to climb to access the slickrock section of this trail. If you do not wish to climb the ladders, hike the loop counterclockwise, gain the slickrock section for the wonderful views, than return the way you came. Visit the caves and artwork afterwards by walking clockwise and return again.

First of two ladders to slickrock section.

GPS	Mile	Elevation	Comment
1	0.00	4,918'	Start Cave Springs Trail.
2	0.13	4,936'	Area of caves
3	0.23	4,942'	Ladders
1	0.70	4,918'	Finish Loop.

Petroglyph in one of the caves; Remnants of ranching life in another cave.

Paul Bunyan's Potty & Tower Ruin

Hikes 27-42

29a
29b

Paul's Potty. *Photo by Tyler & Alene Root.*

29a: To Paul Bunyan's Potty/Return 1

Total Distance	Hiking on road is 6.6 miles RT.
Difficulty Rating	Moderate
Surface	Deep sand on 4x4 road
Gradient	Easy
Average Time	4.5 hours
Elevations	Gain: +121 on road. Negligible on trail
Maps	Trails Illustrated 210: Needles & Island in the Sky National Park Utah

29b: To Tower Ruin/Return 2

Total Distance	Hiking on road is 8.0 miles RT; Trail is 1.2 miles RT.
Difficulty Rating	Moderately Strenuous
Surface	Deep sand on 4x4 road
Gradient	Easy
Average Time	6 hours if hiking road
Elevations	Gain: +154 on road; +39 on trail

Summary

Two very interesting rock formations and ruins are accessible via Salt Creek & Horse Canyon Roads. The actual trails are easy and very short. The problem is that the road has been closed for three years due to extensive and continuous damage by flooding. Attempts to repair it are often quickly washed away again. NPS recommends at least two high-clearance, 4-wheel-drive vehicles go together if the road is open. Access, at the time of this writing, is by foot starting at the locked gate near the start of Salt Creek Road.

Hiking Horse Canyon Road. *Photo by Tyler & Alene Root.*

Directions to Trailhead

From Needles Entrance Station, drive 0.9 miles to the signed turnoff for Cave Springs and Salt Creek. Drive this paved road 0.6 miles to a T junction. Turn left on the gravel road and drive 1.3 miles to Salt Creek Road. Turn right and drive 0.20 miles to the locked gate and park. If the road is passable, you must obtain a permit from the visitor center to unlock the gate.

Trail Description

Tower Ruin is high in the cliff. *Photo by Tyler & Alene Root.*

Due to continuous flooding, many sections of the road are covered in deep sand. That is why we give these hikes a moderate to more strenuous rating. After the gate, hike about 2.5 miles to the junction of Horse Canyon and Salt Creek Canyon Roads ❷. Go left on Horse Canyon. The trail can be tricky to follow as brush and debris continue to interrupt the route direction. Keep following the wash in general. Arrive at Paul Bunyan's Potty ❸ and walk a very short path towards this amazing feature. It is very aptly named! Just below to the left behind a large tree is a well preserved ruin. If you have the energy, go on to Tower Ruin ❹ which is another 0.70 miles up the road. This section is narrow and overgrown which makes for tough walking. From the trailhead, it is 1.2 miles RT to see the ruin which is nestled in a cliff and in excellent condition.

GPS	Mile	Elevation	Comment
1	0.00	4,916'	Start at locked gate on Salt Creek Road.
2	2.50	4,962'	Junction: Go left on Horse Canyon Road; right is Salt Creek Road.
3	3.30	5,047'	Paul Bunyan's Potty, Return 1
4	4.00	5,653'	Tower Ruin TH. Trail is 1.2 miles RT.

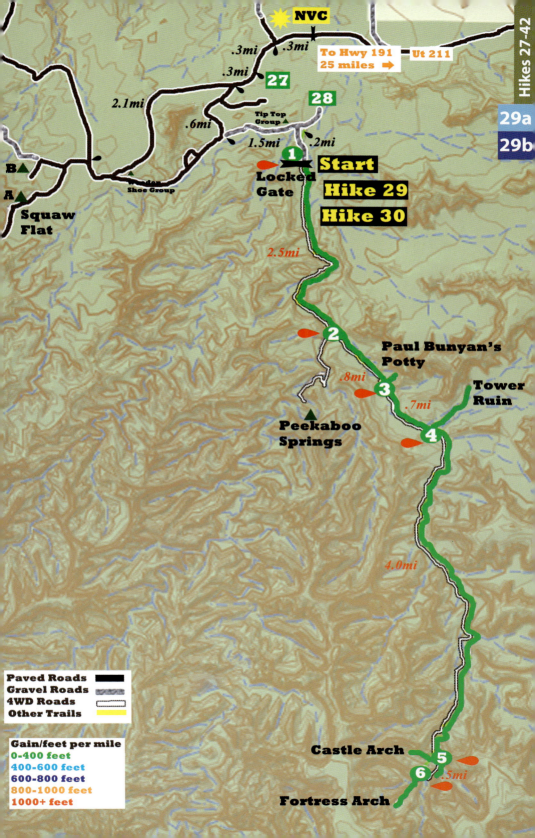

Castle Arch & Fortress Arch

Approaching Castle Arch. *Castle & Fortress Arch photos courtesy of the Natural Arch & Bridge Society: www.naturalarches.org.*

30a: To Castle Arch

Total Distance	16 miles RT on the road; 0.80 miles RT on the trail
Difficulty Rating	Very Strenuous if hiking the road; Easy otherwise
Surface	Road is deep sand, sometimes overgrown with brush.
Gradient	Easy
Average Time	10 hours
Elevations	Gain: On the road is +365; on the trail is +85
Maps	Trails Illustrated 210: Needles & Island in the Sky National Park Utah

30b: To Fortress Arch

Total Distance	17 miles RT on the road; 1.0 miles RT on the trail
Difficulty Rating	Very Strenuous if hiking the road; Easy otherwise
Surface	Road is deep sand, sometimes overgrown with brush.
Gradient	Easy
Average Time	11 hours
Elevations	Gain: On the road is +407; on the trail is +100

Summary

See map on page 157. These are two very interesting arches accessed by easy trails. The problem is that the road has been closed primarily in the spring and fall for three years due to extensive and continuous damage by flooding. Attempts to repair it are often quickly washed away again. NPS recommends at least two high-clearance, 4-wheel-drive vehicles go together if the road is open. If the road is closed to vehicle traffic, these hikes are seriously strenuous. The description assumes the road is closed to vehicles.

Directions to Trailhead

From Needles Entrance Station, drive 0.9 miles to the signed turnoff for Cave Springs and Salt Creek. Drive this paved road 0.6 miles to a T junction. Turn left on the gravel road and drive 1.3 miles to Salt Creek Road. Turn right and drive 0.20 miles to the locked gate and park. If the road is passable, you must obtain a permit from the visitor center to unlock the gate.

Fortress Arch

Castle Arch near end of trail.

View out from under Fortress Arch.

Trail Description

After the gate, hike about 2.5 miles to the junction of Horse Canyon and Salt Creek Canyon Roads ❷. Go left on Horse Canyon. The trail can be tricky to follow as brush and debris continue to interrupt the route direction. Keep following the wash in general. Arrive at Paul Bunyan's Potty ❸ which you can see from the road. It is very aptly named! Go on to Tower Ruin ❹ which is another 0.70 miles up the road. This section is narrow and overgrown which makes for tough walking. It is a very long 4 miles from Tower Ruin to Castle Arch ❺. The sand is deep and tiring. The Castle Arch Trail itself is only 0.80 miles RT. The arch is in view most of the time; it has a similar thin span to Landscape Arch in Arches National Park and is quite delicate. Being very old, its years are also numbered. The trail fades into brush without a defined ending. Another 0.50 miles on the road gets you to the trailhead for Fortress Arch ❻. That trail is 1.0 miles RT. It also is very easy. Fortress Arch is high on the cliff side.

GPS	Mile	Elevation	Comment
1	0.00	4,916'	Start at locked gate on Salt Creek Road.
2	2.50	4,962'	Junction: Go left on Horse Canyon Road; right is Salt Creek Road.
3	3.30	5,047'	Paul Bunyan's Potty
4	4.00	5,653'	Tower Ruin TH. Trail is 1.2 miles RT.
5	8.00	5,280'	Castle Arch TH. Trail is .80 miles RT.
6	8.50	5,320'	Fortress Arch TH. Trail is 1.0 miles RT.

Wooden Shoe Arch Overlook

Wooden Shoe Arch began life about 300 million years ago. Read the story at this overlook.

Wooden Shoe Arch Overlook

Pothole Point Trail

31

A pothole with rain water brings new life. Island in the Sky is in the distance.

Total Distance	0.60 mile loop
Difficulty Rating	Easy
Surface	Slickrock
Gradient	Easy
Average Time	30 minutes
Elevations	TH: 5,067; Gain: +45
Maps	Trails Illustrated 210: Needles & Island in the Sky National Park Utah

Summary

Hike across slickrock covered with potholes that aid the growth of plant life in the desert. A 50 cent brochure available at the trailhead explains the geology of this fascinating process. This is a great walk with children and for folks who wish to walk on easy slickrock. There are no ledges to negotiate. Follow the rock cairns in a short loop; enjoy the spectacular vistas of the Needles, the La Sal Mountains and the deep canyons.

Directions to Trailhead

From Needles Entrance Station, drive 5.0 miles to the signed parking lot for Pothole Point. Facilities: Trash bins.

The Needles are also prominent from this trail.

GPS	Mile	Elevation	Comment
1	0.00	5,067'	Start Pot Hole Point Loop.
2	0.28	5,058'	Lowest point. Good views of Needles.
1	0.60	5,067'	Finish Loop.

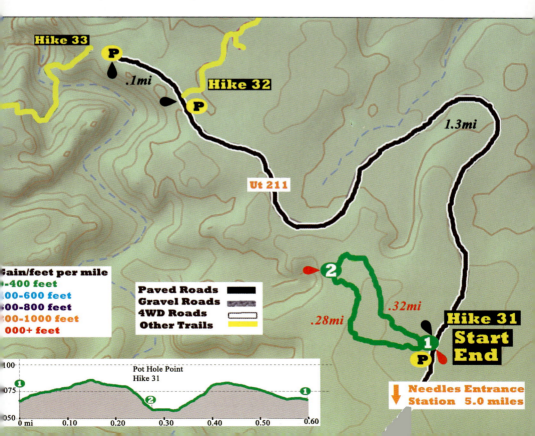

Slickrock Foot Trail

Trail meanders over knolls and slickrock.

Total Distance	2.5 mile loop includes walking out to all four viewpoints
Difficulty Rating	Easy
Surface	Slickrock
Gradient	Easy but with numerous big steps up/down
Average Time	2.5 hours
Elevations	TH: 4,933; Gain: +304
Maps	Trails Illustrated 210: Needles & Island in the Sky National Park Utah

Summary

This is a wonderful hike that stays high on the slickrock and offers stunning 360 degree vistas of the park. Although an easy gradient, there are numerous slickrock ledges with high steps up and down. Follow the loop in either direction and take the extra side trips out to the 4 special viewpoints. The trail is well marked with signs and cairns. A 50 cent brochure at the trailhead describes what you see at the viewpoints.

Directions to Trailhead

From Needles Entrance Station, drive 6.3 miles to the signed parking lot for Slickrock Foot Trail. Facilities: Trash bins.

Trail Description

Always keep an eye open for the cairns marking the twists and turns in the trail and across the slickrock. The trail ascends from the road up through sandy gullies to the slickrock. The first signed junction goes to viewpoint 1 ❷. It is a short spur off to the right that offers a panoramic view to the north and east. Shortly after this viewpoint, hike gradually down slickrock to a split in the trail with a sign that says

Viewpoint 1

Viewpoint 2

Viewpoint 3

Viewpoint 4

"start loop" ③. This description follows the loop counterclockwise. Look for cairns slightly downhill and to the right. Follow along some ledges and come to the signed junction to viewpoint 2 ④. This spur trail is the longest and involves steep steps down. The view of Upper Little Spring Canyon makes a wonderful photo. Back on the main trail, continue climbing, scampering across the undulating slickrock to the signed junction to viewpoint 3 ⑤ which goes slightly downhill from the sign. Here you can view Lower Little Spring Canyon. Viewpoint 4 is also downhill from junction ⑥. Look carefully for cairns here. Walk out to the edge of Big Spring Canyon. Wow! The rock is deep purple. After ⑥, the trail undulates and gradually climbs up to where it soon meets the signed start of the loop at ③. Follow the trail you came out back to your vehicle.

GPS	Mile	Elevation	Comment
1	0.00	4,933'	Start Slickrock Foot Trail.
2	0.23	4,976'	Signed junction to Viewpoint 1
3	0.48	4,959'	Sign: Start loop in either direction. This route goes counterclockwise.
4	0.78	4,933'	Signed junction to Viewpoint 2 which is more off trail and has big steps.
5	1.18	4,968'	Signed junction to Viewpoint 3
6	1.30	4,944'	Signed junction to Viewpoint 4
3	1.92	4,959'	Meet loop sign again. Return to vehicle.
2	2.17	4,976'	Pass junction to viewpoint 1.
1	2.40	4,933'	Finish loop.

Big Spring Canyon Overlook

The Confluence trail begins at this overlook.

Confluence Overlook Trail

The Confluence : Colorado River from the right; Green River from the le[ft]

Total Distance	10.0 miles or any distance RT
Difficulty Rating	Moderate
Surface	A mixture of sand, slickrock and some broken rock
Gradient	Easy with numerous high steps up/down requiring use of hands
Average Time	7 hours
Elevations	TH: 4,918; Gain: +784
Maps	Trails Illustrated 210: Needles & Island in the Sky National Park Utah

Summary

This is a really picturesque and interesting trail that undulates through a variety of terrain including dropping into canyons, hiking across wide grasslands, and slickrock with expansive vistas most of the way. It is also the easiest of the longer distance hikes in the park. Go any distance; it is all enjoyable.

Directions to Trailhead

From the Needles Entrance Station, drive 6.4 miles to the end of the road.

Trail Description

The most difficult section of the hike is right at the trailhead. The route drops moderately steeply into Big Spring Canyon and then climbs right back out to the mesa. A short jaunt across undulating terrain brings you to a ladder at ❷. Just after the ladder, views are quite thrilling. The trail passes through a small keyhole which makes for interesting photography. Hike on the mesa, meandering along ledges for about half a mile before dropping moderately into

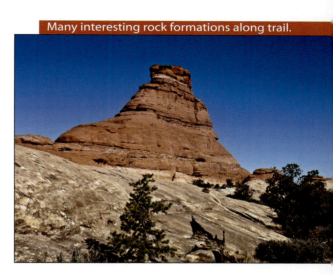

Many interesting rock formations along trail.

Stone mushrooms are plentiful early on in the hike.

- 173 -

Beginning of trail drops into Big Spring Canyon.

Beautiful Elephant Canyon

Hikes 27-42 · 33 · Confluence Overlook Trail

The Keyhole

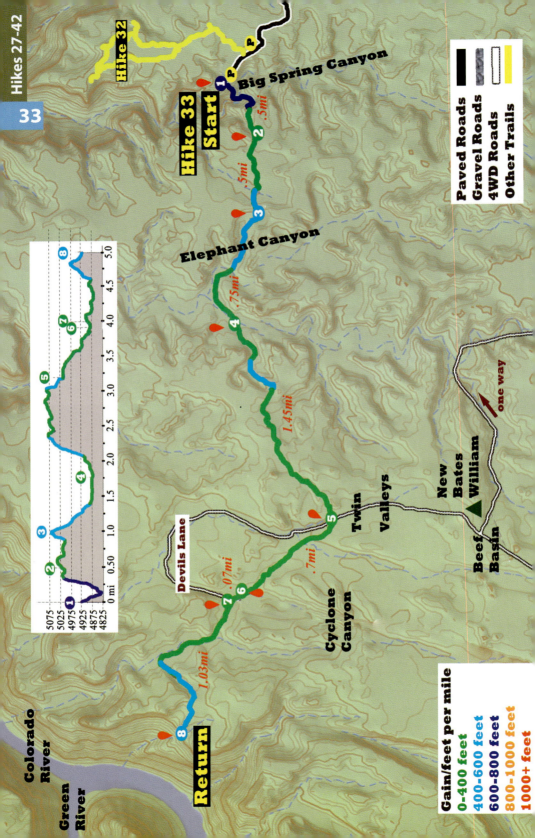

In the bottom of Elephant Canyon, watch for this wash coming in from the right. That is the trail.

Elephant Canyon ❸. Watch carefully for cairns when at the bottom of Elephant Canyon; the trail turns right into a wash ❹. A moderate ascent brings you back to the mesa top and crosses over into Twin Valleys, a very picturesque, wide, grassy drainage. Here you cross Devil's Lane Road for the first time ❺. The trail continues descending gently almost 0.70 mile arriving at a sign that says 1.1 more miles to the confluence ❻. Very shortly the trail crosses the Devil's Lane Road again in lovely Cyclone Canyon. Look south for a stunning view of the Needles. Here the trail follows a road (not the Cyclone Canyon spur) to a pit toilet and picnic tables. From there, it is about another 0.50 miles to the confluence overlook which provides a magical view of the mighty Colorado River absorbing the Green River.

GPS	Mile	Elevation	Comment
1	0.00	4,918'	Start Confluence Overlook Trail.
2	0.50	4,947'	Ladder. Keyhole is shortly after.
3	1.00	5,059'	Start descent into Elephant Canyon.
4	1.75	4,798'	Trail turns right into small wash. Look for cairns. Easy climb to mesa top from here.
5	3.20	4,989'	Cross Devil's Lane Road.
6	3.90	4,866'	Sign says confluence overlook in 1.1 mile.
7	3.97	4,872'	Cross road again. Beautiful views down Cyclone Canyon of Needles.
8	5.00	4,932'	Confluence Overlook. Return.

Peekaboo Springs Options

34a
34b
34c

34a: To Peekaboo Saddle/Return 1

Total Distance	3.5 miles RT
Difficulty Rating	Easy but with one steep scramble with hands up slickrock ledges
Surface	Sandy wash and steep slickrock
Gradient	Easy except for one very short scramble up to reach the saddle
Average Time	1.75 hours
Elevations	TH: 5,099; Gain: +378
Maps	Trails Illustrated 210: Needles & Island in the Sky National Park Utah

Peekaboo Saddle

Hikes 27-42

34a
34b
34c

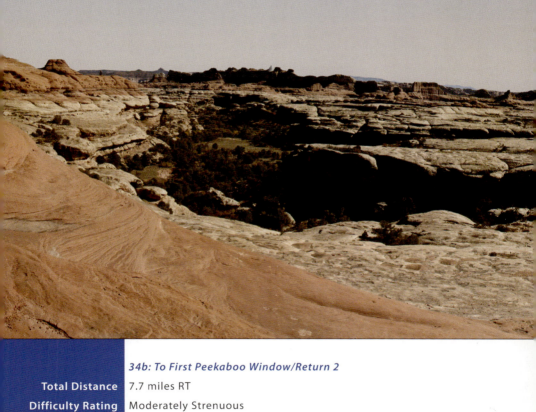

34b: To First Peekaboo Window/Return 2

Total Distance	7.7 miles RT
Difficulty Rating	Moderately Strenuous
Surface	Sandy wash and steep slickrock
Gradient	Ranges from Easy to Steep
Average Time	5 hours
Elevations	TH: 5,099; Gain: +1467

Peekaboo ladder just below saddle.

34c: To Peekaboo Camp/Return 3

Total Distance	10.0 miles Loop
Difficulty Rating	Strenuous
Surface	Slickrock steps, deep sand in wash, road bed, and desert soil
Gradient	Very Steep descent for 0.75 miles, Easy on Hogback Ridge, steep road descent, Easy in wash
Average Time	7 hours
Elevations	TH: 6,253; Gain: +2258

Summary

This is such a marvelously scenic trail, you can go any distance and return. We suggest two interesting return points: one from Peekaboo Saddle which is really just the high point before dropping down into Lost Canyon, and the second from the first peekaboo window. Hikers who go on to the Peekaboo camp are usually spending a night.

A narrow ledge to negotiate

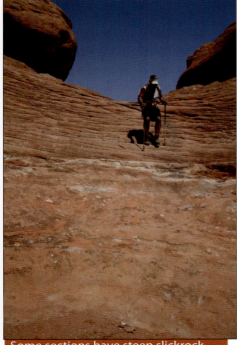
Some sections have steep slickrock.

Directions to Trailhead

From Needles Entrance Station, drive 3.0 miles to the signed turnoff for Squaw Flats Campground. When the road forks, take the left fork through campground A to the parking lot TH. Parking space for RVs. Facilities: Water, pit toilet, trash, recycle.

Trail Description

The signage on the trail is clear and easy to follow although there are sections where attention is required to keep on track with the cairns across slickrock. From the trailhead most of the way to the saddle at ❹, the trail is flat or undulates over slickrock mounds. The very last bit to the saddle requires scrambling up steep ledges of slickrock. The 360 degree views from the saddle include the Las Sal Mountains, south Six-shooter Peak and the Lost Canyon drainage. Not to be missed! Drop into Lost Canyon drainage after the saddle via a short ladder ❺. Pass the signed junction to Lost Canyon ❻ and soon after, LC1 camp at ❼. Now the more serious climbing begins as the trail ascends steep slickrock. Be sure to look back behind you for wonderful views of the La Sal Mountains. This is our favorite part of the trail! Negotiate along ledges, in and around deep canyons until reaching the first peekaboo window ❽. Ascend and descend again to get to the second window ❾. From there, it is downhill 336 feet to Peekaboo Camp ❿.

First Peekaboo

One of many wonderful views

GPS	Mile	Elevation	Comment
1	0.00	5,099'	Start loop at Squaw Flats Campground TH in campground A.
2	0.10	5,097'	Signed junction to Big Spring Canyon Trail. Go straight ahead (SE) for Peekaboo. Right (SW) is Big Spring Canyon Trail.
3	1.10	5,054'	Signed junction to Squaw Canyon Trail. Go straight ahead (SE) to Peekaboo Springs. Left (SW) is Squaw Canyon Trail.
4	1.75	5,231'	Peekaboo Saddle
5	1.98	5,155'	Ladder
6	2.60	5,037'	Signed junction to Lost Canyon Trail. Go straight (SE) to Peekaboo Springs. Right (SW) is Lost Canyon Trail.
7	2.70	5,061'	LC1 camp
8	3.85	5,274'	First Peekaboo window
9	4.15	5,289'	Second Peekaboo window
10	5.00	5,042'	Peekaboo Springs Camp

Squaw Canyon/ Big Spring Canyon Loop

Hikes 27-42
35

View down upper Squaw from saddle

Total Distance	7.1 mile loop
Difficulty Rating	Moderate with steep steps down & up around saddle
Surface	Sand wash and slickrock
Gradient	Mostly Easy
Average Time	4 hours
Elevations	TH: 5,099; Gain: + 1181
Maps	Trails Illustrated 210: Needles & Island in the Sky National Park Utah

Summary

This is one of the shorter and easier loops in Needles Park. It travels primarily through two thickly vegetated canyons with moving streams in the spring and great fall color in October. The route crosses a high saddle with delicious views for a special treat.

Descent into Big Spring has some steep slickrock.

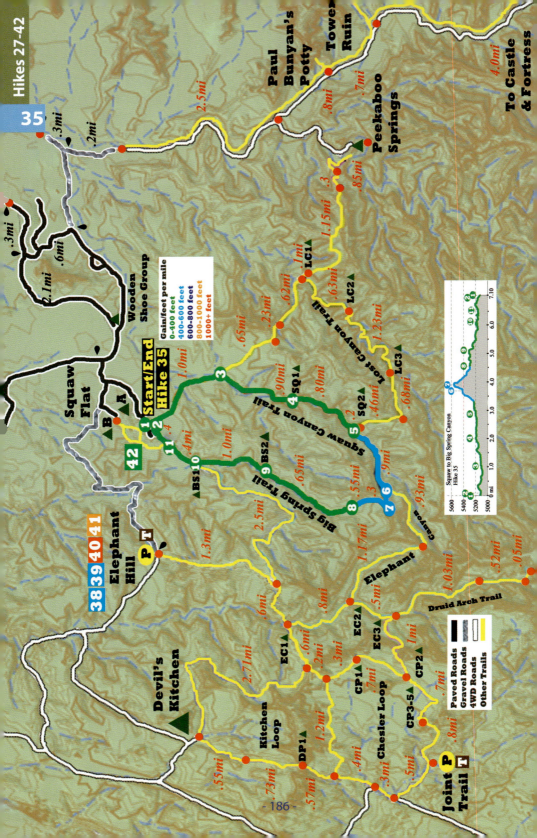

Directions to Trailhead

From Needles Entrance Station, drive 3.0 miles to the signed turnoff for Squaw Flats Campground. When the road forks, take the left fork through campground A to the parking lot TH. Parking space for RVs. Facilities: Water, pit toilet, trash, recycle.

Trail Description

You can hike this route in either direction with no discernible difference. We hike it clockwise. The trail undulates through open country with wonderful views of buttes, spires and distant peaks all the way to the junction at ❸ where you go right into Squaw Canyon. The canyon is wide and meandering at first, gradually getting more narrow. Views are limited by the vegetation and canyon walls. Pass SQ 1 campsite at ❹ to the signed junction to Druid Arch ❺. Keep going straight following directions to Druid Arch; do not cross the creek to your left. In another .30 miles, the trail begins the climb to the saddle between Squaw, and Big Spring Canyons. This section is very scenic as it ascends from the sandy wash on slickrock to the junction with Elephant Canyon at ❻. Go right here and continue climbing to the saddle between Squaw and Big Spring Canyons ❼, where the view is all encompassing. The descent from the top has some very steep steps down which may require use of hands. Still, the views of Big Spring Canyon are superb from this high vantage point. The descent ends by entering the Big Spring wash at ❽ and follows it all the way past BS 2 camp ❾ to BS 1 camp and the junction to Chesler Park ❿. The canyon is very picturesque. From the Chesler junction back to the parking lot, the trail opens up considerably to show off the marvelous red rock features of Canyonlands National Park.

GPS	Mile	Elevation	Comment
1	0.00	5,099'	Start loop at Squaw Flats Campground TH in campground A.
2	0.10	5,097'	Signed junction with Big Spring Canyon Trail. Go straight ahead (SE) for loop. Right (SW) is Big Spring Canyon Trail.
3	1.10	5,054'	Signed junction with Peekaboo Trail. Go right (SW) for Squaw Canyon. Left is Peekaboo Trail.
4	2.00	5,085'	SQ 1 campsite
5	2.80	5,189'	Signed junction to Druid Arch Trail. Go straight ahead (SW) towards Druid Arch for this loop. Do not go left (S) across creek. That is Lost Canyon Trail.
6	3.70	5,405'	Signed junction with Big Spring Trail. Go right for this loop. Left goes to Elephant Canyon.
7	4.00	5,550'	Big Spring Saddle
8	4.55	5,261'	Trail enters wash at bottom of descent.
9	5.20	5,125'	BS 2 camp
10	6.20	5,115'	Signed junction to Chesler Park & BS1 Camp. Go straight ahead.
11	6.60	5,148'	Signed junction with Loop B campground. Go straight for loop A starting point.
2	7.00	5,097'	Signed junction with Peekaboo Trail. Go left to parking lot.
1	7.10	5,099'	End loop at Squaw Flats Campground TH in campground A.

Big Spring/Elephant Canyon Loop

Hikes 27-42

36

Ascending to top of Big Spring Canyon

Total Distance	10.3 mile loop
Difficulty Rating	Strenuous
Surface	Deep sand, packed sand, broken rock, slickrock, some bouldering, ladders
Gradient	Easy & Moderate but with numerous big slickrock ledges requiring use of hands
Average Time	7-8 hours
Elevations	TH: 5,099; Gain: +2259 ft
Maps	Trails Illustrated 210: Needles & Island in the Sky National Park Utah

Summary

This loop climbs and descends many times offering a tremendous variety of scenery from intimate, lushly vegetated canyons to high vistas, slot canyons, and grassy flats. It offers a total park experience.

Directions to Trailhead

From Needles Entrance Station, drive 3.0 miles to the signed turnoff for Squaw Flats Campground. When the road forks, take the left fork through campground A to the parking lot TH. Parking space for RVs. Facilities: Water, pit toilet, trash, recycle.

Trail Description

Immediately after leaving the parking lot, the trail forks at a signed junction to Big Springs Canyon ❷. Go right and hike in easy undulating, open grasslands for about a mile passing the signed junction to Squaw campground Loop B at ❸. This is a lovely section of trail with lots of red buttes, spires and distance peaks attracting your attention. At ❹, is the signed junction to Chesler Park Trail which is your return route. For now, go left and soon cross over into Big Spring Canyon which is lush and open in the lower reaches. Pass BS 2 camp ❺. There are numerous times when hiking up this wash the route meanders in and out. There are cairns along the side as well as in the wash itself which is confusing. At about mile 2.55 watch carefully for

View back down into Squaw Canyon

Elephant Canyon

the trail to leave the wash to the left and start climbing up slickrock ❻. From here, the trail takes on an entirely different character. It alternates from climbing slickrock to entering numerous large bowls several times. On the final ascent to the top at ❼, there are several places where long legs are a distinct advantage in negotiating the very high steps up! From this high point, enjoy wonderful views back into Big Spring Canyon and Squaw Canyon. The trail drops steeply from here to the signed junction to Squaw Canyon ❽. Go right here. The next 2 miles is our favorite section of the trail. A ladder ❾ assists hikers up the steep slickrock. Enter a narrow slot and cross into Elephant Canyon. The trail follows along ledges before dropping to the valley floor and meeting the signed junction to Druid Arch ❿. Continue straight

Hikes 27-42

36

Slot between Big Spring & Elephant Canyon

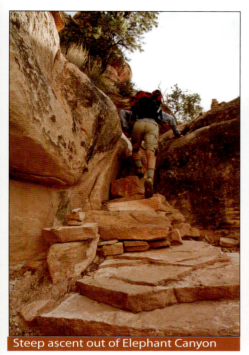
Steep ascent out of Elephant Canyon

A delightful small canyon near the top

ahead. EC 2 camp will be on your left. Follow the wash and cairns. As usual, there are often confusing routes going in and out of the wash. Just continue following its direction but keep an open eye for the next signed junction with Chesler Park Trail. There is a sign at this junction for EC1 camp as well ⑪. Turn right out of the wash and begin the climb out of Elephant Canyon. Here is another fascinating section of

On Chesler Trail near junction to Squaw Flats Campground

Last leg on route to Squaw Flats

trail, climbing ledges and steps and passing through narrow slots. From here to the end of this loop, the trail undulates constantly through a wondrous variety of rock formations, little canyons, and expansive vistas. Turn right at the signed junction to Elephant Hill parking lot ⑫ and left at the junction with the Big Spring Trail ❹. You are now back in familiar territory and on your way to Squaw Flat campground A loop parking lot. For a much shorter hike along this latter section of scenic trail, see hike 38, Elephant Hill to Squaw Flat Campground.

GPS	Mile	Elevation	Comment
1	0.00	5,099'	Start loop at Squaw Flats Campground TH in campground A.
2	0.10	5,097'	Signed junction to Big Spring. Go right (SW) for loop. Straight ahead is Peekaboo & Squaw Canyon Trails.
3	0.50	5,148'	Signed junction to Squaw Flats campground B; continue southwest.
4	0.90	5,115'	Signed junction to Chesler Park Trail. Go left (S) up Big Spring for this loop. Chesler (SW) is the return trail. BS 1 camp near junction.
5	1.90	5,125'	BS 2 camp
6	2.55	5,261'	Watch for cairns. The trail leaves wash to the left and starts climb up slickrock.
7	3.10	5,526'	Top of Big Spring Saddle
8	3.40	5,376'	Signed junction to Squaw Canyon. Go right (SW) for loop; left (E) is Squaw Canyon Trail.
9	4.33	5,484'	Ladder at top of Elephant Pass
10	5.50	5,222'	Signed junction for Elephant Canyon & Druid Arch. Continue straight (N) for this loop. EC 2 & 3 camps nearby.
11	6.30	5,147'	Signed junction: A bit confusing. Chesler Park is left (W). Go right (N) out of the wash on good trail but no confirming sign. Start steep climb up. EC 1 camp nearby.
12	6.90	5,350'	Signed junction to Elephant Hill parking lot (N). Go right (E) for this loop towards Squaw Flats campground.
4	9.40	5,115'	Signed junction: Big Spring Trail to right (S). Go straight (NE) for parking lot.
3	9.80	5,148'	Signed junction to Squaw campground Loop B. Go straight for A parking lot.
2	10.20	5,097'	Signed junction: Peekaboo Trail to right (S). Go left (N) to parking lot.
1	10.30	5,099'	Squaw Flats Campground parking lot on loop A

Squaw Canyon/Lost Canyon Loop

37

Total Distance	8.60 mile loop
Difficulty Rating	Moderate
Surface	Soft sand, packed sand, broken rock, slickrock
Gradient	Mostly Easy but with steep slickrock ledges to negotiate
Average Time	5.5 hours
Elevations	TH: 5,099; Gain: +1352 ft
Maps	Trails Illustrated 210: Needles & Island in the Sky National Park Utah

Summary

This is primarily a loop through two lushly vegetated canyons. A magnificent high saddle separates the two canyons and offers big views, slickrock hiking and some use of hands to ascend/descend ledges. Lost Canyon feels wild and remote.

View from Peekaboo saddle towards Squaw Flats Campground

37

Directions to Trailhead

From Needles Entrance Station, drive 3.0 miles to the signed turnoff for Squaw Flats Campground. When the road forks, take the left fork through campground A to the parking lot TH. Space for RVs. Facilities: Water, pit toilet, trash, recycle.

Trail Description

We like to hike this loop counterclockwise, starting up Squaw Canyon and coming back Lost Canyon. Arriving at the top of Lost Canyon Saddle from this direction is nothing but awesome. Yes, the trail really does drop to the bottom! We also like

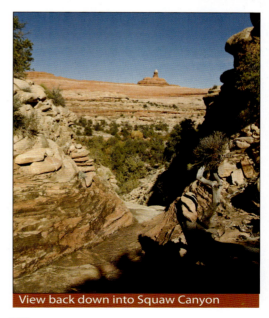
View back down into Squaw Canyon

Hikes 27-42

37

Lost Canyon Saddle looking down into Lost Canyon

Hikes 27-42

37

Ascending the narrow canyon to the saddle

The descent into Lost Canyon is steep

returning the very scenic Peekaboo section in the late afternoon when the light is better for photos. Squaw Canyon is lushly vegetated. In spring the creek runs fresh; in fall the Cottonwoods contrast the red canyon walls. Just before reaching SQ 2 campsite ❻, there is an unmarked fork in the trail. The true route goes straight ahead; the left fork is a shortcut that seems to be developing. Turn left at the signed junction to Druid Arch ❺ and cross the creek. As soon as you pass SQ 2 ❻, the trail begins ascending through a fantastic, narrow canyon. The trail is in the slickrock stream. Once through this, it is open vistas across slickrock to the high saddle ❼. This is our favorite view on the loop. The idea of dropping all the way to the bottom of this picturesque canyon is mind blowing. Watch very carefully for

Lost Canyon opens up near LC2 camp

Ladder to Peekaboo Saddle

cairns to guide you down. It is steep in places and requires use of hands. Once off the slickrock, the canyon remains very narrow, twisting and wild, gradually widening. It is lush and cool; the stream runs briskly in the spring. At the signed junction to Peekaboo Springs, go left ❿; the trail stays just a little longer in the canyon bottom before starting the ascent to Peekaboo Saddle. Slickrock ledges may require use of hands. There is a short ladder at ⓫. The trail tops out at Peekaboo Saddle ⓬ with 360 degree views. Then, watch again for cairns as the trail drops down off the steep slickrock. The trail back to the parking lot climbs and descends over two more slickrock buttes and can be a bit tiring in the afternoon heat. Still, the views are the reward!

GPS	Mile	Elevation	Comment
1	0.00	5,099'	Start loop at Squaw Flats Campground TH in campground A.
2	0.10	5,097'	Signed junction with Big Spring Canyon Trail. Go straight ahead (SE) for loop. Right (SW) is Big Spring Canyon Trail.
3	1.10	5,045'	Signed junction with Peekaboo Trail. Go right (SW) for Squaw Canyon. Left is Peekaboo Trail.
4	2.00	5,085'	SQ 1 campsite
5	2.80	5,189'	Signed junction to Druid Arch Trail. Go left (S) across creek on Lost Canyon Trail. Straight ahead (SW) goes to Druid Arch.
6	3.00	5,188'	SQ 2 campsite
7	3.46	5,407'	Lost Canyon Saddle
8	4.14	5,166'	LC 3 campsite
9	5.37	5,093'	LC 2 campsite
10	6.00	5,037'	Signed junction to Peekaboo Springs. Go left (NW) for loop. Right (SE) goes to Peekaboo Springs.
11	6.62	5,155'	Ladder
12	6.85	5,231'	Peekaboo Saddle
3	7.50	5,045'	Signed junction to Squaw Canyon. Go straight ahead (N) to parking lot.
2	8.50	5,097'	Signed junction. Go straight ahead (N) for parking lot.
1	8.60	5,099'	Finish loop.

Elephant Hill to Squaw Flats Campground

From Elephant Hill to the junction to Squaw : The Needles

Total Distance	4.7 miles one way
Difficulty Rating	Moderate
Surface	Slickrock with some ledges and steps up
Gradient	Ranges between easy and moderate with one steep climb at beginning
Average Time	3.5 hours
Elevations	TH: 5,116; Gain: +960
Maps	Trails Illustrated 210: Needles & Island in the Sky National Park Utah

Summary

This is an incredibly scenic trail with a lot of variety. It provides an excellent sampling of the typical features in Needles Park as the trail undulates in, over and around this striking topography.

Directions to Trailhead

From Needles Entrance Station, drive 3.0 miles to the signed turnoff for Squaw Flats Campground. Turn left; at the first fork in the campground road, turn right following signs to Campground B & Elephant Hill. From this junction, drive 2.8 miles to the end of the road, (which turns to gravel in the campground). There are narrow spots and blind curves, but any vehicle can drive this section of the road. Park at the designated Elephant Hill parking lot. Facilities: Pit toilets, trash bins.

This section is filled with interesting rock formations.

After the junction enjoy wide vistas.

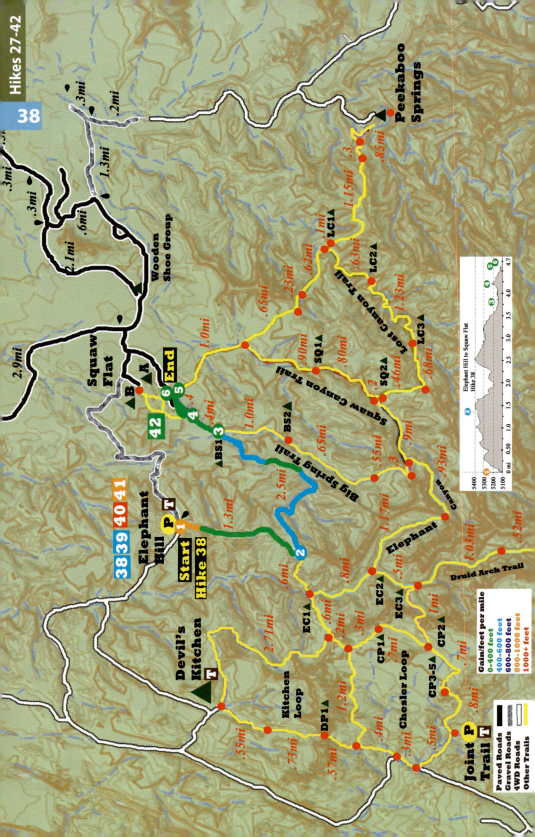

Hikers on the last leg back to Squaw Flats

Trail Description

The trail begins with a short but breath-taking climb up slickrock steps. Then it cruises for a while along edges of canyons shoulder by red buttes, winding and twisting through small dunes of slickrock. What a pleasure! Expansive vistas, narrow slots keep the camera busy. When you come to the first signed junction at ❷, turn left towards Squaw Flat Campground. Straight ahead goes to Chesler Park and Devil's Kitchen. The trail takes a moderate dive and subsequent climb as the entertainment continues. There are too many delightful sights to mention all the way to ❸ where the trail meets up with Big Spring Canyon Trail. Then it travels through more grassland with open vistas to the parking lot at Squaw Flat Campground loop A.

GPS	Mile	Elevation	Comment
1	0.00	5,116'	Start at Elephant Hill parking lot.
2	1.30	5,332'	Signed junction to Chesler, Druid, Squaw Flats Campground. Go left (E).
3	3.80	5,115'	Signed junction with Big Spring Trail. Go straight ahead.
4	4.20	5,148'	Signed junction to loop B in Squaw Flat Campground
5	4.60	5,097'	Signed junction with Peekaboo Trail. Go left to finish.
6	4.70	5,099'	Finish at Squaw Flat Campground loop A.

Druid Arch

Druid Arch

Total Distance	9.6 miles RT
Difficulty Rating	Moderate
Surface	Slickrock, big steps down & up, packed and soft sand
Gradient	Ranges from Easy to steep
Average Time	6 hours
Elevations	TH: 5,116; Gain: +1,775
Maps	Trails Illustrated 210: Needles & Island in the Sky National Park Utah

Summary

Druid Arch is different; it recreates feelings of Stonehenge! It follows the scenically diverse trail to Elephant Canyon and then turns into the pretty wash surrounded by wonderful rock formations all the way to a viewpoint of the arch high above.

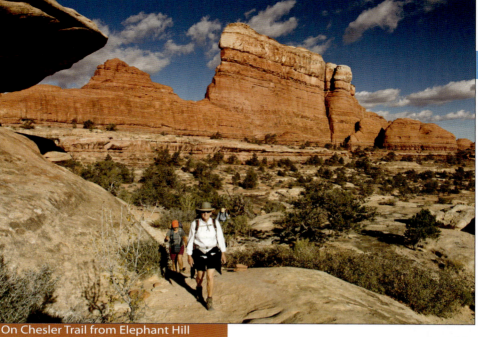
On Chesler Trail from Elephant Hill

The Needles

Small canyon on way to Elephant wash

Directions to Trailhead

From Needles Entrance Station, drive 3.0 miles to the signed turnoff for Squaw Flats Campground. Turn left; at the first fork in the campground road, turn right following signs to Campground B & Elephant Hill. From this junction, drive 2.8 miles to the end of the road, (which turns to gravel in the campground). There are narrow spots and blind curves, but any vehicle can drive this section of the road. Park at the designated Elephant Hill parking lot. Facilities: Pit toilets, trash bins.

The final approach to Druid Arch starts to get steep.

Trail Description

The beginning of the trail follows the same route as Hike 38, continuing past the signed junction to Squaw Flats Campground at ❷. The trail continues to undulate over slickrock and passes through what we like to call Mini Chesler Park, a grassy area surrounded by massive rock walls. Not far beyond this meadow, the trail passes through a narrow notch and enters the Elephant Canyon area. Soon, the trail plunges into a narrow slot which is the beginning of the steep descent to Elephant Canyon wash ❸. Go left; the trail is on the opposite bank of the wash from where you entered it and clearly marked with a sign. The canyon is rugged, surrounded by fascinating rock formations. In 0.8 miles, you will come to the signed junction to Big Spring Canyon. Go right here. EC2 & EC3 camps are near this junction. The trail continues alternating from the wash to the bank. At ❺ is the signed junction to Chesler Park. (This is a very difficult 1.0 mile route, more an adventure than a trail as there are many places where hands are necessary to negotiate boulders and ledges.) In about another mile, watch for the trail to leave the main wash and enter a smaller canyon off to the left ❻. It is marked with a cairn, but still is easy to miss if you are not looking for it. The trail gets much steeper towards the very end. Climb a ladder ❼ and you are just about at the viewpoint ❽.

Descending to Elephant wash

GPS	Mile	Elevation	Comment
1	0.00	5,116'	Start Druid Arch at Elephant Hill parking lot.
2	1.30	5,332'	Signed junction to Chesler, Druid, and Squaw Flats Campground. Go straight ahead.
3	1.90	5,134'	Elephant Canyon wash signed junction to Chesler; Druid Arch; EC1 campsite. Go left up Elephant Canyon wash on the right bank of wash.
4	2.70	5,216'	Signed junction to Big Spring: Take the right fork (S). Left fork goes over Elephant saddle to Big Spring & Squaw Canyon trails.
5	3.20	5,313'	Signed junction to Chesler and Joint Trail. Continue straight south.
6	4.23	5,377'	Confusing spot. Big cairn marks the trail exits the big wash and enters a smaller wash to the left.
7	4.75	5,565'	Ladder
8	4.80	5,705'	Druid Arch viewpoint

Chesler Park Options

40a
40b

Chesler Park

40a: To Chesler Park Overlook

Total Distance	5.40 miles RT
Difficulty Rating	Moderately Strenuous
Surface	Slickrock; big steps up/down, some use of hands
Gradient	Ranges from Easy to Very Steep
Average Time	4 hours
Elevations	TH: 5,116; Gain: +1700
Maps	Trails Illustrated 210: Needles & Island in the Sky National Park Utah

40b: Chesler Park Loop

Total Distance	10.3 mile loop
Difficulty Rating	Very Strenuous
Surface	Slickrock; big steps up/down, some use of hands
Gradient	Ranges from Easy to Very Steep
Average Time	8 hours
Elevations	TH: 5,116; Gain: +2548

Descending to Elephant Canyon

Hikes 27-42
40a
40b
Chesler Park Options

Trail back out of Elephant Canyon

Summary

Chesler Park is the most famous and popular trail in Needles Park. It is scenically thrilling from the very start all the way around, hence, hikers can go out and back any distance that suits their time and fitness and experience the best Needles Park has to offer. Don't miss this hike because of the loop's total distance.

Directions to Trailhead

From Needles Entrance Station, drive 3.0 miles to the signed turnoff for Squaw Flats Campground. Turn left; at the first fork in the campground road, turn right following signs to Campground B & Elephant Hill. From this junction, drive 2.8 miles to the end of the road, (which turns to gravel in the campground). There are narrow spots and blind curves, but any vehicle can drive this section of the road. Park at the designated Elephant Hill parking lot. Facilities: Pit toilets, trash bins.

Scenic vistas are constantly changing.

Trail Description

The trail begins with a serious upward thrust, climbing high rock steps for the first quarter mile before undulating across a fascinating area of rock towers and views into Big Spring Canyon. The Needles are already visible to the south. Best photos are in the morning hours. At ❷, the trail forks, the left going to Squaw Flats campground on a very picturesque route; see hike 38 for details. The trail continues to undulate over slickrock and passes through what we like to call Mini Chesler

Mini Chesler Park

Entering the famous slot

Park, a grassy area surrounded by massive rock walls. Not far beyond this meadow, the trail passes through a narrow notch and enters the Elephant Canyon area. Soon, the trail plunges into a narrow slot which is the beginning of the steep descent to Elephant Canyon wash ❸. The steps down are very high in places. This section of trail through the canyon is wild looking, rough and tumble, with twists and turns that keep the visual thrills constantly changing. A sign at ❹ marks the turnoff to Devil's Kitchen, a route we describe in hike 41. For this loop, there is one more big climb up through the needles above you. Again, some steps are very high. Once at the top, a very short descent through sand brings

After the slot offers different perspectives of the Needles.

you to the signed beginning of the Chesler loop trail ❺. This makes a good return point for a shorter hike of 5.40 miles total. The views of Chesler Park from here are magical, the expanse is immense. To continue the loop, we take the left fork and hike clockwise. A long, relatively easy undulating stretch through sandy soil makes a big loop around the eastern edge of the park. Pass CP1 at ❻ and continue through easy descending, open country to the signed junction to Druid Arch ❼. This mile

Close up to the Needles on last leg of loop

long trail to Druid is more an adventure than a hike as much terrain is traversed with the help of hands and butts! Just south of the Druid junction is the short spur trail to CP3-5 camps followed quickly by CP2. At the southeastern corner of the park, the trail suddenly drops into a deep slot. This is the beginning of the Joint. Just before climbing down, look for a trail sign ❽ to a viewpoint off to the east. This viewpoint offers a closer look at the fascinating needles although to get there requires some exposed ledge walking.

Hiking through The Joint is amazing. It's a long narrow slot about a quarter mile long. Some places require scrambling over boulders. There is a "cave" that hikers have adorned with thousands of rock cairns. When you come out, the trail drops steadily through a boulder field until finally reaching the 4x4 road ❾. Walk down this road, taking the right fork when it splits at ❿ and watch for a sign on the right bank ⓫ that shows where to leave the road and continue on the loop. It is a long climb with some steep sections requiring use of hands. The trail winds through boulders and cracks and clambers over slickrock. It's a little bit like being an ant maneuvering through a bowl of gumdrops. At ⓬ is the signed junction to Devil's Kitchen and Chesler. Go right towards Chesler for another 1.2 miles of undulating, picturesque terrain, Once back at ❺, retrace your route back to Elephant Hill parking lot. What a day!

GPS	Mile	Elevation	Comment
1	0.00	5,116'	Start Chesler Park at Elephant Hill parking lot.
2	1.30	5,332'	Signed junction to Chesler, Druid, Squaw Flats Campground. Go right (W).
3	1.90	5,134'	Elephant Canyon wash signed junction to Chesler; Druid Arch; EC1 campsite. Go straight ahead (W) across wash and begin steep climb.
4	2.50	5,465'	Signed junction to Chesler & Devil's Kitchen. Take the left fork (S) for Chesler and ascend the steep trail through the needles.
5	2.70	5,568'	Signed junction: Begin Chesler Loop by going clockwise taking the left fork. Right is the return route and also our route for Devil's Kitchen loop.
6	3.00	5,635'	CP 1 campsite
7	3.70	5,631'	Signed junction to Druid Arch. Continue straight ahead (SW).
8	4.40	5,587'	Descend into the joint. Also a great viewpoint of Needles about 500 yards out to the left. Some scrambling necessary to gain viewpoint.
9	5.20	5,322'	Trail meets the 4x4 road. Pit toilet & picnic tables. Walk west on road.
10	5.70	5,247'	Road forks. No signage. Take the right fork and continue on road another 0.25.
11	6.00	5,201'	Signed junction to Devil's Pocket just off road right. Leave road and follow this trail to continue on Chesler loop.
12	6.40	5,395'	Signed junction to Devil's Kitchen; go right (E) to continue Chesler loop.
5	7.60	5,568'	Back at beginning of Chesler loop. Go left (N) uphill.
4	7.80	5,465'	Signed junction to Devil's Kitchen. Go right (N) to trailhead.
3	8.40	5,134'	Signed junction at Elephant Canyon wash. Continue straight and begin steep climb out.
2	9.00	5,332'	Signed junction to parking lot and Squaw Flat CG. Go straight (N).
1	10.30	5,116'	Finish at Elephant Hill parking lot.

Devil's Kitchen Loop

Total Distance	10.9 mile loop
Difficulty Rating	Strenuous
Surface	Sand, slickrock and sections with high steps up/down
Gradient	Ranges from Easy to Very Steep
Average Time	6.5 hours
Elevations	TH: 5116; Gain: + 2614
Maps	Trails Illustrated 210: Needles & Island in the Sky National Park Utah

View of Pinnacle Formation from DP1 in Devil's Pocket

Summary

This is an exciting and extremely beautiful loop that, although marked as Strenuous, is much easier than the Chesler loop. Yet, you still hike through a section of Chesler Park and have amazing views all the way through the entire loop. Hike any distance out and back for shorter options.

Directions to Trailhead

From Needles Entrance Station, drive 3.0 miles to the signed turnoff for Squaw

On Chesler Trail near Elephant Hill

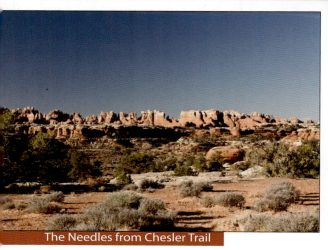

The Needles from Chesler Trail

Flats Campground. Turn left; at the first fork in the campground road, turn right following signs to Campground B & Elephant Hill. From this junction, drive 2.8 miles to the end of the road, (which turns to gravel in the campground). There are narrow spots and blind curves, but any vehicle can drive this section of the road. Park at the designated Elephant Hill parking lot. Facilities: Pit toilets, trash bins.

Trail Description

The first 2.70 miles are the same as the Chesler loop hike 40. It begins with a serious upward thrust, climbing high rock steps for the first quarter mile before undulating across a fascinating area of rock towers and views into Big Spring Canyon. The Needles are already visible to the south. Best photos are in the morning hours. At ❷, the trail forks, the left going to Squaw Flats campground on a very picturesque route. See hike 38 for details. The trail continues to undulate over slickrock and passes through what we like to call Mini Chesler Park, a grassy area surrounded by massive rock walls. Not far beyond this meadow, the trail passes through a narrow

Entering the big joint above Elephant Canyon

View of the notch into Chesler from Devil's Kitchen junction

Trail out of Elephant Canyon

notch and enters the Elephant Canyon area. Soon, the trail plunges into a narrow slot which is the beginning of the steep descent to Elephant Canyon wash. The steps down are very high in places. The canyon is wild looking, rough and tumble, with twists and turns that keep the visual thrills constantly changing. A sign at ❹ marks the turnoff to Devil's Kitchen; this trail is your return route. For now, go left on the Chesler Trail and begin the steep climb through the Needles. Once at the top, a very short descent through sand brings you to the signed beginning of the Chesler loop trail ❺. This makes a good return point for a shorter hike of 5.40 miles total. The views of Chesler Park from here are magical, the expanse is immense. To continue the Kitchen loop, go right at this junction as left goes all the way around Chesler. This section of trail undulates and winds around many fascinating rock formations. The trail gets very close to some of the towering buttes. Meet another junction at ❻. Left goes to the 4x4 Elephant Hill Road. Go right. Soon you will pass through a narrow slot and enter a completely different basin. This is wonderful stuff! Ahead you can see the great Pinnacle Formation. The trail goes right through them, climbing up to a saddle ❼ with super views behind and ahead into Devil's Pocket basin.

The trail towards Devil's Kitchen is filled with needle formations.

Twisting canyons of stone mushrooms last leg of loop

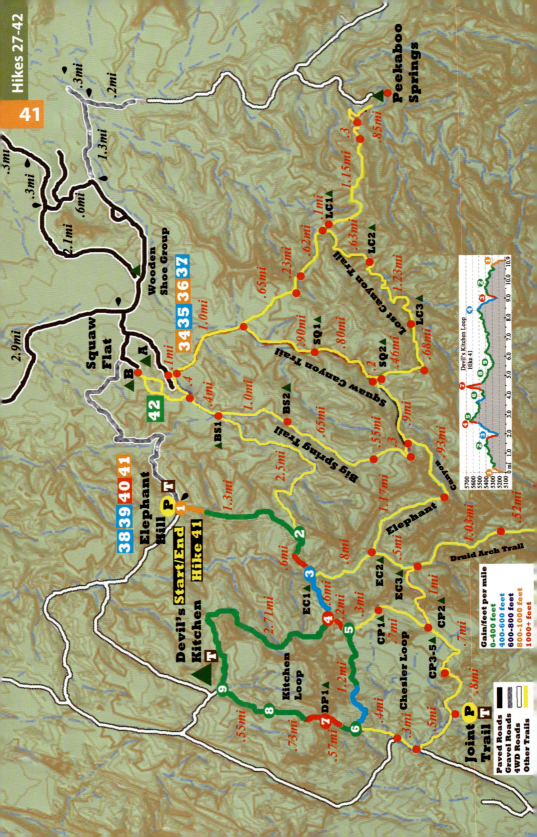

Trail goes through the Pinnacle Formation.

Down you go, than saunter easily across the wide sandy floor of the basin, passing DP1 camp ❽ and meeting the Elephant Hill 4x4 road at Kitchen Camp ❾. This entire basin is completely surrounded by dramatic red sandstone walls. It's a winner! Once at the road, walk towards the pit toilet to find the ongoing trail heading off to the right (E). Don't take the road! Here begins a fascinating section of trail that climbs easily and negotiates through giant stone mushrooms and other interesting formations. Now views are to the north of the La Sal Mountains. Hike along multiple deep canyons, many adorned with more stone mushrooms. Once back at junction ❹, retrace your steps to the parking lot. It is still another 2.5 miles home, and remember there is some steep climbs yet ahead.

GPS	Mile	Elevation	Comment
1	0.00	5,116'	Start Devil's Kitchen at Elephant Hill parking lot.
2	1.30	5,332'	Signed junction to Chesler, Druid, and Squaw Flats Campground. Go straight ahead.
3	1.90	5,134'	Elephant Canyon wash signed junction to Chesler; Druid Arch; EC1 campsite. Go straight ahead (W) across wash and begin steep climb.
4	2.50	5,465'	Signed junction to Chesler & Devil's Kitchen. Take the left fork for Chesler and ascend the steep trail through the needles. Right hand fork is the return route.
5	2.70	5,568'	Signed junction to Chesler & Devil's Kitchen. Begin Devil's Kitchen Loop by turning right. Left is the route for Chesler Loop.
6	3.90	5,395'	Signed junction to 4x4 road and Devil's Kitchen. Go straight ahead for Devil's Kitchen. Left comes from Chesler Loop and the jeep road.
7	4.47	5,559'	High saddle between Chesler and Kitchen Basins. Views! Descend steeply into Devil's Pocket.
8	5.20	5,310'	DP 1 campsite. Grassy basin surrounded by stone needles and mushrooms.
9	5.75	5,214'	Meet Elephant Hill 4x4 road. Do not walk the road. Look for trail off to the east near the pit toilet on the east end of the road.
4	8.46	5,465'	Signed junction to Chesler & Devil's Kitchen. Go left for parking lot.
3	9.06	5,134'	Elephant Canyon wash signed junction to Chesler; Druid Arch; EC1 campsite. Go straight ahead (W) across wash and begin steep climb.
2	9.66	5,332'	Signed junction to Chesler, Druid, and Squaw Flats Campground. Go straight ahead.
1	10.96	5,116'	Finish at Elephant Hill TH.

Squaw Flats Campground Loops

42a
42b
42c

42a: Loop A to Big Spring Trail back to A

Total Distance	1.20 mile loop
Difficulty Rating	Easy but with ledges and a cable
Surface	Slickrock
Gradient	Easy but with short moderately steep sections on slickrock
Average Time	1 hour
Elevations	TH: 5099 ; Gain: + 253
Maps	Trails Illustrated 210: Needles & Island in the Sky National Park Utah

View from the top

42b: Loop B to Big Spring Trail back to B

Total Distance	1.55 mile loop
Difficulty Rating	Easy but with ledges and a cable
Surface	Slickrock
Gradient	Easy but with short moderately steep sections on slickrock
Average Time	1.25 hours
Elevations	TH: 5071; Gain: + 250

Hikes 27-42

42a 42b 42c

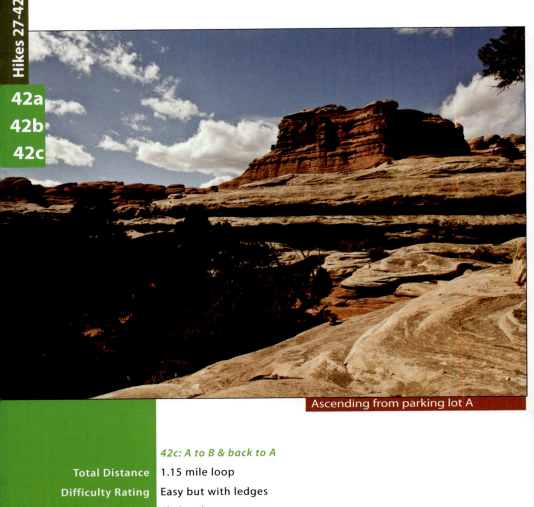
Ascending from parking lot A

42c: A to B & back to A

Total Distance	1.15 mile loop
Difficulty Rating	Easy but with ledges
Surface	Slickrock
Gradient	Easy but with short moderately steep sections on slickrock
Average Time	1 hour
Elevations	TH: 5071; Gain: +206

Summary

These are not official trails for Needles Park, but they should be! They are marvelous, short excursions into the buttes between loop A & B in Squaw Flats Campground. Put together your own loops. Our favorites are from Loop A or B to Big Spring Trail and back. There are ledges and a cable to negotiate on these routes.

Directions to Trailhead

42a: From Needles Entrance Station, drive 3.0 miles to the signed turnoff for Squaw Flats Campground. When the road forks, take the left fork through campground A to the parking lot TH. Parking space for RVs. Facilities: Water, pit toilet, trash, recycle. 42b: From Needles Entrance Station, drive 3.0 miles to the signed turnoff for Squaw Flats Campground. When the road forks, take the right fork and immediately the next left fork into B loop.

Trail Description

Both 42a & b hikes climb a short section of slickrock with the aid of a cable, climb to a high viewpoint and descend through a narrow slot between two big boulders. If you prefer not to climb the cable, go directly from A to B and back (42c) and skip the route to Big Spring Trail. See the chart below for specific instructions.

Entering the slot from loop B

Route from loop B

Climbing with the cable

GPS	Mile	Elevation	Comment
42a: Loop A to Big Spring Trail			
1	0.00	5,099'	Start Trailhead A to Big Spring Loop at trailhead A parking lot.
2	0.20	5,148'	Signed junction: to B loop is right. Go left to Big Spring Trail.
3	0.40	5,209'	Unmarked junction: right through slot goes to B loop. Go straight ahead to cable.
4	0.45	5,239'	Cable
5	0.60	5,274'	Slot through rock
6	0.70	5,148'	Signed junction. Go left to parking lot. Right is Big Spring Canyon.
1	1.20	5,099'	Finish loop at trailhead A parking lot.
42b: Loop B to Big Spring Trail			
7	0.00	5,071'	Start Loop B in Campground B parking lot.
3	0.35	5,209'	Unmarked junction at end of slot: go right to cable. Left goes to A parking lot.
4	0.40	5,239'	Cable
5	0.55	5,274'	Slot through rock
6	0.65	5,148'	Signed junction. Go left to parking lot A. Right is Big Spring Canyon.
1	1.15	5,099'	Trailhead A parking lot. Cross road to continue to B.
2	1.35	5,148'	Signed junction: Go right to B loop. Left goes to cable & Big Spring Trail.
7	1.55	5,071'	Finish loop at trailhead B parking lot.
42c: A to B to A loop (or hike in reverse)			
1	0.00	5,099'	Start Trailhead A to B Loop at trailhead A parking lot.
2	0.20	5,148'	Signed junction: to Loop B is right.
7	0.40	5,071'	Loop B parking lot. Continue back to A. Go left uphill.
3	0.75	5,209'	Unmarked junction at end of slot. Go left to A parking lot. Right goes to cable.
2	0.95	5,148'	Signed junction: Go right to A loop. Left goes to Loop B.
1	1.15	5,099'	Finish loop at trailhead A parking lot.

Appendix A: Entrance Fees/Addresses/Park Regulations

Entrance Fees are the same for both parks.
$10 per vehicle for a 7 day pass; $5 per bicyclist, motorcycle, or walker

The following passes can be used at both parks:
1. Interagency Annual Pass ($80/yr) Previously the Golden Eagle/National Park Pass
   - Available to anyone.
   - Allows free entry to National Parks, Fish and Wildlife Refuges, Bureau of Land Management, Bureau of Reclamation and Forest Service sites that charge fees.
2. Interagency Senior Pass ($10 lifetime) Previously the Golden Age Pass
   - Available to U.S. citizens sixty-two years and older.
   - Free entrance to all federal fee areas;
   - 50% discount on some camping, activity and other special user fees
3. Interagency Access Pass (Free) Previously the Golden Access Pass
   - Available to permanently disabled U.S. citizens
   - Free entrance to all federal fee areas
   - 50% discount on some camping, activity and other special user fees
4. Interagency Annual Military Pass (Free)
   - Available to qualifying active military and their dependents
   - Present military ID card at entrance gates
5. Local Pass: ($25/year)
   - Available to anyone
   - Free entrance to Arches, Canyonlands, Hovenweep and Natural Bridges

Arches National Park
PO Box 907
Moab, UT 84532
435-719-2299
E-mail: archinfo@nps.gov
www.nps.gov/arch

Canyonlands National Park
2282 SW Resource Blvd.
Moab, UT 84532
435-719-2313
E-mail: canyinfo@nps.gov
www.nps.gov/cany

Canyonlands Natural History Association is a non-profit organization established to assist the scientific and educational efforts of the land management agencies of the Colorado Plateau. They select the quality educational materials, both free and purchased, for all the visitor center outlets and other agency contact stations. Bookstore sales are the parks primary source of income as federal agency funding declines.
Become a Member. Enjoy the benefits of a 15% discount on purchases of $1 or more:
2282 SW Resource Blvd., Moab, UT 84532
435-259-6003; 800-840-8978
www.cnha.org

Bureau of Land Management
82 East Dogwood, Moab, UT 84532
435-259-2100
www.blm.gov/ut/st/en.html

Dead Horse State Park
PO Box 609, Moab, UT 84532
435-259-2614 General Information
800-322-3770 Camping reservations
www.reserveamerica.com   Camping reservations

Regulations
- Backcountry Permits are required for all backcountry activities; reservations are recommended.
- Group Camping Permits and reservations are required for all group camps.
- Pets are not allowed on hiking trails at overlooks or in the backcountry (even in vehicles). They must be leashed at all times. They may be walked along paved roads and may accompany owners in the park campgrounds. There are kennel services in Moab. Though they are free to go on trails in the surrounding public lands, it is recommended to keep them on a leash to avoid damage to the fragile biological crusts.
- Bicycles are not allowed on hiking trails or off road.
- ATVs are not allowed in the parks. All motorcycles must be street legal.
- See Appendix C for additional backcountry regulations.

Appendix B: Camping

In Arches National Park

1. **Devil's Garden Campground (NPS)**
    - 18 miles inside the park from the Arches Entrance Station
    - 52 sites/reservations required between March 1st and October 31st through National Recreation Reservation Service
    - Book online at www.recreation.gov
    - Or call 1-877-444-6777 (518-885-3639 International)
    - Reservations must be made at least 4 days ahead up to 6 months in advance
    - $20 per site per night; all Federal passes apply
    - Tables & fire rings
    - Water & flush toilets in various locations. No showers
2. **Arches National Park Group Campsites (NPS)**
    - 11 people or more
    - $3 per person per night with a $33 per night minimum
    - Reservations required through www.recreation.gov
        - Juniper Basin: up to 55 people
        - Canyon Wren: up to 35 people

In or Near Island in the Sky District, Canyonlands National Park

3. **Willow Flats (NPS)**
    - 7.4 miles inside the park from Island in the Sky Entrance Station
    - 12 sites. Designed for tents and small RVs maximum length 28 feet
    - First-come, first-served

Appendix B: Camping, continued

- $10/site. All Federal passes apply
- No water; pit toilets, trash disposal, picnic tables, fire rings

4. **Dead Horse Point State Park_ Kayenta Campground**
   - On Hwy 313 about 18 miles from Hwy 191 junction. At the signed junction to Dead Horse State Park, drive Hwy 313 about 7.5 more miles to the campground
   - 21 sites with numerous sites for large RVs
   - Most sites are reservable: call Utah State Parks at 800-322-3770 at least two days in advance or go to: http://www.reserveamerica.com/camping/Dead_Horse_Point_State_Park
   - $20/ site for partial hookup

5. **Cowboy Camp (BLM)**
   - On Hwy 313 about 18 miles from Hwy 191 junction
   - 6 primitive sites; no water
   - First-come, first-served
   - $10/site; Interagency Senior & Access passes are half-price

6. **Horsethief Campground (BLM)**
   - On Hwy 313 about 12 miles from Hwy 191 junction
   - 56 sites with numerous sites for large RVs
   - First-come, first-served
   - $15/site per site. Interagency Senior & Access passes are half-price
   - Pit toilets, trash disposal, picnic tables, fire rings; no water

7. **Lone Mesa Group Site (BLM)**
   - On Hwy 313 about 9 miles from Hwy 191 junction
   - 5 sites
   - Lone Mesa A- 15 to 30 people; Lone Mesa B- 15 to 30 people; Lone Mesa C- 15 to 40 people; Lone Mesa D- 10 to 20 people; Lone Mesa E- 15 to 30 people. $20 reservation fee, $4/person/night. Interagency Senior & Access passes are half-price. Reservations: 435-259-2100

Public Campgrounds around Moab

1. **Sand Flats public campsites (Grand County)**
   - From the junction for the Moab Visitor Center on Center Street and Hwy 191, go 1 block north to 100 North. Turn right (east). Proceed ½ mile and turn right onto 400 East. Go ½ mile and turn left at Dave's Corner Market onto Millcreek Drive. Proceed for ½ mile to stop sign. Go straight at stop sign onto the Sand Flats Road that continues up a hill for 2 ½ miles to the Entrance Booth
   - 120 sites
   - Pit toilets, some fire rings and picnic tables; no water
   - First-come, first-served
   - $10/vehicle up to 5 people; $2/extra person; $2/towed vehicle trailer. No passes
   - Group sites available. No water. $50-$60 for 16-20 people. $10 Reservation fee Reservations: Grand County 435-259-2444

BLM campgrounds around Moab

BLM public lands are good alternatives to the parks for visitors with pets and ATV's or other off-road type vehicles. Pets are allowed on trails, campgrounds, and back country roads. They administer over 3000 miles of back country roads, many of which are very popular for 4-wheel-drive vehicles, ATV's, UTV's, etc and are quite scenic. Riding off-road is not allowed in most places. For more information & maps with campground locations, contact the BLM office in Moab: 82 East Dogwood, Moab, UT 84532, 435-259-2100, www.blm.gov/ut/st/en.html.

1. **Hwy 128 public campsites**
    - Hwy 191 & 128 junction is 2.4 miles north of the Moab Visitor Center
    - 12 campgrounds with a total of 100 sites
    - All on the Colorado River
    - Pit toilets & fire rings; no water
    - First come, first served
    - $15/site. Interagency Senior & Access passes are half-price
    - Group Camps at: Goose Island A- 15 to 25 people; Goose Island B- 20 to 40 people. Both are $20 reservation fee, $4 per person per night. Big Bend A- 25 to 40 people; Big Bend B- 15 to 20 people; Big Bend C- 15 to 30 people. Each has a $20 reservation fee and $4 per person per night. No water. Reservations: BLM 435-259-2100
2. **Hwy 279 Potash Road public campsites**
    - Hwy 191 & 279 junction is 3.9 miles north of Moab Visitor Center
    - Three campgrounds with a total of 33 sites
    - All on the Colorado River
    - Pit toilets & fire rings; no water
    - First-come, first-served
    - Jaycee Park $15/site, Williams Bottom $10/site, and Goldbar $10/vehicle Interagency Senior & Access passes are half-price
    - Gold Bar has Group sites. No water. Reservations: BLM 435-259-2100
3. **Kane Creek Road public campsites**
    - Four campgrounds with a total of 50 sites
    - Primitive sites with pit toilets & fire rings; no water
    - First come, first served
    - King's Bottom: 11 sites at $15/site, Moonflower (8 sites) and Hunter Canyon (13 sites) are both $10/site, and the Ledge with 18 sites is $10/vehicle. Interagency Senior & Access passes are half-price
4. **Ken's Lake**
    - 10 miles south of Moab along the La Sal Mountain Loop
    - 31 sites with numerous sites for large RVs
    - Pit toilets, trash, picnic tables, fire rings; no water
    - $15/site. Interagency Senior & Access passes are half-price
    - First come, first served

Private Campgrounds in and around Moab

There is an abundance of private campgrounds and RV parks in and around Moab: www.discovermoab.com/campgrounds_private.htm.

Appendix B: Camping, continued

In or Near Needles District, Canyonlands National Park

1. **Squaw Flats Campground (NPS)**
   - 3.0 miles inside the park
   - 27 sites with numerous sites for large RVs
   - 2 wheel chair sites
   - First-come, first-served
   - $15/site. All Federal passes apply
   - Water, flush and pit toilets, trash disposal, recycling, picnic tables, fire rings
2. **Needles Group Sites inside the park (NPS)**
   - Reservations required. Non refundable $30 fee; send by mail or by fax no less than 2 weeks in advance; Reservation form obtained at the park entrance, visitor center, or: www.nps.gov/cany/planyourvisit/backcountrypermits; E-mail: canyinfo@nps.gov. Mail: Reservation Office 2282 S West Resource Blvd. Moab, UT 84532 435-259-4351; Fax: 435-259-4285
   - 11 person minimum; maximum stay of 7 days
   - $3 per person per night. Passes apply if not being used to reach the minimum
     - Squaw Flat Group Site: up to 50 people and 10 vehicles
     - Wooden Shoe Group Site: up to 25 people and 5 vehicles
     - Split Top Group Site: up to 15 people and 3 vehicles

BLM sites around Needles

BLM public lands are good alternatives to the parks for visitors with pets and ATV's or other off-road type vehicles. Pets are allowed on trails, campgrounds, and back country roads. They administer over 3000 miles of back country roads, many of which are very popular for four 4-wheel drive vehicles, ATV's, UTV's, etc and are quite scenic. Riding off-road is not allowed in most places. For more information & maps with campground locations, contact the BLM office in Moab: 82 East Dogwood, Moab, UT 84532, 435-259-2100, www.blm.gov/ut/st/en.html.

1. **Lockhart Basin** is 5 miles before (east) the Needles Entrance Station on Hwy 211. Turn north on Lockhart Basin Road. There are about 40 undeveloped sites scattered along the road. The road is two-wheel-drive as far as Indian Creek; four-wheel-drive beyond. Hamburger Rock, about 1 mile from the turnoff, has 8 developed sites with pit toilet, picnic tables & fire rings; no water. Fees & passes apply
2. **Creek Pasture** is 7 miles before (east) the Needles Entrance Station on Hwy 211. Turn north on the dirt road. About 10 undeveloped sites with a few picnic tables. No water; waste disposal bags provided (donation suggested); no fee. High clearance two-wheel-drive road
3. **Superbowl** is 8 miles before (east) the Needles Entrance Station on Hwy 211. Turn south on the dirt road. Go through gate and drive .4 miles. About 10 undeveloped sites; no services; no water; waste disposal bags provided (donation suggested). No fee. High clearance two-wheel-drive road
4. **Bridger Jack Mesa** is 14 miles before (east) the Needles Entrance Station on Hwy 211. Turn south on Beef Basin/Elk Mtn. Road. Cross creek. Drive .8 miles; take the first right (west) and drive another .9 miles to designated campsites. 21 sites;

no services; no water; waste disposal bags provided (donation suggested); no fee. High clearance two-wheel-drive road
5. **Wind Whistle** is 50 miles from Needles Entrance Station. It is on the Needles Overlook Road which is 6 miles north of Hwy 211 & Hwy 191 junction. Drive the paved Needles Overlook Road 6 miles to Canyon Rims Recreation Area. 17 developed sites; pit toilets; picnic tables, fire rings. Fees & passes apply

Private Campgrounds near Needles

Needles Outpost is .3 miles before (east) the Needles Entrance Station on Hwy 211. Six people/site/2 vehicles or 1RV at $20/night; $3 for showers; group sites by reservation only; $10/person/night; fire pits, picnic tables, potable water; pets on leash. There is a general store with groceries, books, maps, camping supplies etc. Gas (no diesel). Reservations: needlesoutpost@aol.com; PO Box 1107, Monticello, UT 84535, 435-979-4007.

Appendix C: BackcountryRegulations/Permits/Camping

In 1995 the NPS published a new backcountry plan for Canyonlands National Park because of significant increase in backcountry use. In order to protect the fragile desert environment, the following regulations were established:

1. No pets allowed in the backcountry, not even in vehicles.
2. No wood gathering or wood fires allowed in the backcountry.
3. In 2010 Congress passed a law allowing firearms in National Parks following all state laws and permits. They are not allowed inside any federal building including Visitor Centers. Firearms may be carried into the backcountry with a valid permit. However discharging a firearm is prohibited.
4. No disturbing or entering archaeological or historical sites. No collecting artifacts or natural features. No disturbing, hunting, or feeding wildlife.
5. No swimming or bathing allowed except in the Colorado and Green Rivers, and Salt Creek.
6. Specific backpacking campsites designated for:
    - Syncline Loop at Island in the Sky
    - All the Needles hiking trails
    - Upper Salt Creek drainage
7. At- large camping allowed in specific zones
    - Backpackers may choose their own low- impact site
    - They must camp at least one mile from the nearest road or trail or established campsite
    - Minimum 300 feet from any water source except Colorado & Green Rivers
    - Minimum 300 feet from any archeological site
8. All backpacking & 4x4 camping sites must obtain a permit; fees apply. Reservations are recommended but not required. Campsites and permits not reserved in advance are available on a first-come, first-served basis at district visitor centers the day before or the day of a trip. Permits are issued up to one hour before the close of business each day.

Appendix C: Backcountry, continued

- Non refundable $30 fee; send by mail or by fax no less than 2 weeks in advance Reservation form available at www.nps.gov/cany/planyourvisit or at visitor centers. Call 435-259-4351 or E-mail: canyinfo@nps.gov
    - Mail reservation to: 2282 S West Resource Blvd. Moab, UT 84532
    - Fax reservation to: 435-259-4285
- Beginning in 2014 reservations can be made based on availability up to 4 months in advance and walk in permits will only be issued based on availability at the time. The most up to date information on the reservation process will be available at www.nps.gov/cany/planyourvisit or by calling the reservation office at 435-259-4351.

9. Backpacking stays are limited to 14 consecutive days /trip; 7 days in any one zone. Group size limited to 7; low- impact camping; pack out all trash; visitor centers at Island in the Sky and Needles have detailed information on these sites.
10. 4x4 stays are limited to 3 nights/vehicle; group size limited to 10 for Needles, 15 for Island in the Sky. Backpackers may stay at designated vehicle campsites in both the Needles District and Island in the Sky District only if the site is reserved and included on the visitors permit Backpackers with a permit for a camp at- large zone may not camp in a vehicle campsite. Backpackers must pack out all trash and may not leave it in the pit toilets.
11. Visitor Centers at Island in the Sky and Needles have detailed information on all these sites.
12. 4x4 backcountry day use fee is $10/vehicle. All revenue from the sale of these permits is used to recover the costs associated with providing the permits and protecting park resources.

Hike 41: Devil's Kitchen Loop in the Needles District

Meet the Authors

Anne and Mike Poe have been adventuring together since their marriage in 1970. From whitewater kayaking to glacier skiing, to bicycling for six months at a time, their adventures began to expand more and more. In the 1980's Anne started writing and photographing all their trips so the memories would always stay fresh. She published numerous articles in various outdoor magazines.

In 1984, they bicycled from Costa Rica to Peru. In successive years, they bicycled from Alaska to Idaho; six months through New Zealand; six months around Australia; and finally, in 1997, a six month odyssey from Bali, Indonesia to Hong Kong, China. Anne wrote her first book, *On Our Own: A Bicycling Adventure in Southeast Asia*, about that amazing journey. It is currently for sale on Amazon.com in print as well as in Kindle format.

From 1984 to 1990, they instructed downhill skiing in Vail, Colorado. During the summer months, they instructed Outward Bound Courses in the Boundary Waters Wilderness area of northern Minnesota.

By 1990, backpacking Canada's wilderness trails became the new focus. For six summers, they returned to explore new areas, photograph, and write.

In 2004, they started hiking Colorado's more than 4,000 miles of trails. When they went to Crested Butte, they knew they had found a hiker's paradise. For four summers, they researched, hiked, photographed and mapped this marvelous area, and produced their first guidebook: *Crested Butte Colorado: 60 Scenic Day Hikes*. When that sold out the first summer, before just printing another edition, they made revisions suggested by their followers and came out with the second edition: *Crested Butte Colorado: 65 Scenic Day Hikes*. The book is a hot item in local stores as well as in REI and on Amazon.com.

Summer 2010, they hiked trails in Silverton & Ouray, Colorado with the intention of producing another book. They knew the area's potential from having hiked many of the area trails over the years. In spring of 2011, they introduced their latest title: *Southwest Colorado: High Country Day Hikes*. You will find it in many stores in Silverton & Ouray as well as in REI and on Amazon.com

All those years in Colorado, they spent the off seasons of April, May, and October in Moab, Utah hiking trails for this, their newest publication: *Utah National Parks, Arches and Canyonlands Day Hikes*. Hikers from all over continue to be enthusiastic about this new style of hiking guides that the Poe's are producing. So, put your boots on and go take a hike! The information you need is in your hands.

Visit their website, www.hikingbikingadventures.com to see all their adventures in photos, books and magazine articles.

To offer feedback or comments, and for updated trail information go to: Facebook.com/takeahikeguidebooks.

Anne is an Alpha. Alpha-1 is a lung emphysema that is inherited. It is progressive and life-long. She had lost 30% of her lung capacity before the disorder was discovered and abated through augmentation therapy. There are only 10,000 Americans currently diagnosed correctly, with a potential 100,000 possible cases. An estimated 20 million Americans are carriers of the abnormal genes. At risk groups include chronic COPD, irreversible asthma, and emphysema sufferers. Her goal is to bring awareness of the disorder to a public place. For more information, go to www.alpha-1foundation.org.

Also by Anne & Mike Poe

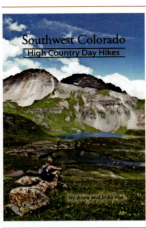

Southwest Colorado High Country Day Hikes
by Anne and Mike Poe
Published Spring 2012

Includes 60 scenic hikes in Ouray, Silverton and Crested Butte, Colorado. Available for purchase in local stores in Ouray, Silverton, Durango, Ridgway, Montrose and Telluride. Also available at REI and on Amazon.com.

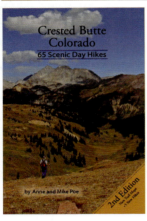

Crested Butte Colorado 65 Scenic Day Hikes
by Anne and Mike Poe
2nd Edition Published Spring 2012

One book devoted just to the incredibly scenic trails in Crested Butte. Available for purchase in many Crested Butte stores, in Gunnison, Ouray, Silverton, Durango, Ridgway, Montrose and Telluride. Also available at REI and on Amazon.com.

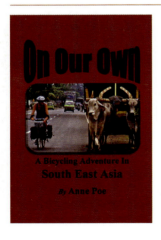

On Our Own: A Bicycling Adventure in Southeast Asia
by Anne and Mike Poe
Published Spring 2011

An 8,000-mile journey by bicycle through the heart of Southeast Asia. Available on Amazon.com in paperback and kindle formats.

Become our fan on facebook: facebook.com/takeahikeguidebooks